EVERYBODY WANTS TO BE LOVED

—

POEMS

DON EDWARDS

author HOUSE

AuthorHouse™
1663 Liberty Drive
Bloomington, IN 47403
www.authorhouse.com
Phone: 833-262-8899

Published by AuthorHouse 01/30/2023

ISBN: 978-1-7283-7845-9 (sc)
ISBN: 978-1-7283-7844-2 (e)

Print information available on the last page.

I have wrung another batch of thoughts from my dry dishrag of a brain
And in the doing have suffered great harm to my ability to comprehend.
Every time I think, I am undermined again.

VOLUME ONE

If I Were Beautiful Like You

If I were beautiful like you
I would live in Manhattan or sometimes L.A.
And walk my dog down 5th Avenue in the latest fashion jeans
Or lounge upon the beach in little but well-designed clothing

If I were beautiful like you
I would attend the finest events looking happy to be there
And be photographed always smiling in the newest of couture
Moving gracefully across the floor without a stumble

If I were beautiful like you
I would have a family with one maybe two children
And I would mother them up whenever I could
And leave them well provided for when I had to be away

If I were beautiful like you
I would busily move forward daily with constant smiles and many followers
And I'd be considerate of others less perfect because that's beauty too
In fact it's a requirement so that beauty may endure

Go Alone

When you're going everywhere you go on your own
Just tell your friends you'd rather be alone than be with me

If you think that dark is better than the light
If you'd rather be cold than have the warmth
If a bed of thorns beats the cuddling up
If crickets are better than the human voice
If against the wind is how you walk
Then I guess you'd rather go it alone

But remember that —

The world is not a companion
But a place to wander upon

Night is not for sleeping
And alone will define your day
So if you'd rather be without than with me
Then you can just go away

Be careful what you wish for
Because I'll be gone and we'll be through
And the way things are
No one is coming for you

It's just easier not to be alone
Better to have that lover to fan your life's flame
It's not a good reason — I know it isn't
But it's a reason just the same

I Guess Everybody Wants To Be Loved

My great grandfather married his younger cousin
And they had children of their own
Other than this little tic I get right here
That sparks and twitches all down my spine
I think their wedding worked out just fine
I guess everybody wants to be loved

A wedding ring upon a bone that was a finger
Love shared between two doomed to fail
Time eats all that enter into this place
So nothing remains here but the love

She was a golden goddess from Clemmons
Who had a way with her lips that just beat it all
I was only a redneck kid from Catawba
Hanging on helpless as she made me fall
At least she kept me around for a little
I guess everybody wants to be loved

A wedding ring upon a bone that was a finger
Love shared between two doomed to fail
Time eats all that enter
So nothing remains but the love

Now I love a dream that rises to meet me in the evening
From the darkness she stares raptor-like untamed and free
I can only look back in silent wonder
She's the most beautiful creature any god ever made
I can't imagine why she comes to me
I guess everybody wants to be loved

A wedding ring upon a bone that was a finger
Love shared between two doomed to fail
Time eats all that enter
So nothing remains but the love

Loneliness is a disease that will quietly surrender
When the right and loving partner rises up to you
Love will save your feet and hands and give you glory
Only you may know but that will be enough
Don't forget that everybody wants to be loved

Everybody wants to be loved

I Would Have Poetry

IG is watching
Everyone is keeping score
Your life is a news story
Your life's not your own anymore

I would have poetry in my life
The Peeping Tom photos of the paparazzi will not do
I want words that sing of love and beauty
Enough already of twitching hindquarters
More like death throes they are than passion

Give me a startling high of romance instead
Mount pure and private love with me and ride swift through life's dirty
poisoned streets
Above and over without regard for the day's foibles or its predatory requirements

Come with me, ignore distraction, and feel how nearly perfect the light of
love can be
Life is a dream of your own making
Build it of love and pass through this muddy world with me

You could have done better
Now I'm not sure what to do
Hey baby
Hey baby
Hey baby hey
What you gonna do now

Could it be you — it looked of you — she moved as you
But you say you are waiting quiet for my return
What I have seen must be a trick of electric light no doubt your head imposed
upon another's body — because you wait for me, right

How can I love without you
How can my dream be if you turn away
Where is there for me to run to
Only you can light my lonely day

The beauty of your eyes give to me
If I am allowed to gaze there, then you may distribute the rest where you will
I would spend a lifetime in the elegance of those eyes
And never feel want or loss
Live and love then until the tears come
And that will be enough for me.

The Origin Of Love

You say you don't understand
That you're alone and without a plan
I think you should look around
At this world of constant beauty
Look close and it'll be found
Where love comes from

There's a reason behind the fact
There's a rose before the scent
That which can only be imagined
From the rainbow arced above
All that you may determine to be
Where love comes from

That illumination behind you
Is what makes you to be you
No matter how your bones are covered
A sense of light beneath the darkness
And a song hidden by the silence
Announces where love comes from

If you will see trust in the vacant air
Then you can find it easy
To see the reason that all is so
We will see what happens when
Lights are lit by passion
And our lives take on the magic glow

Listen to the cries among the laughter
Watch the raindrops feed the thirsty flowers
All is a balance of living freely given
Up and down, left and right, back and forth
This world of plenty is ours
It's where love comes from

That which breathes behind the veil
Guides daily with a gentle hand
Occasionally shoving the dawdler
Or caressing the tired and dirty forgotten one
There is much to curse or sing for
This is the place love comes from

My Mama Was An Orphan

My mama was an orphan with no money for me
A young woman with dreams of being some day
Of finishing school and having a home
I'd a been an anchor to weigh her down too much
So she gave me away

Like an old couch with a rip or a dog that won't hunt
I was sent off to someone with the money to pay
She showed me her back as she walked out the door
Determined to have her own life to create as she went
People been doing that to me right up until today

It's hard to be a partner to someone you don't expect to stay
I still remember a mother who wouldn't take and hold my hand
When I look at you I see the beauty that I want to be inside
But I can't touch you without imagining you soon will turn aside
Sorry I just can't get over being left behind

Life requires change as it spins along its course
What is supposed to will be you can't deny
No one close to me can remain as the days flow in and out
Desire cools and floats up above like prayers into the sky
So don't expect me to carry you when I fly

I'd rather say it first than to wait for your goodbye
I don't like surprises or being shown the way to the door
So lets enjoy this time and hold each other close tonight
And figure I'll be gone before you can say you don't want me anymore
I know it must be coming as it always has before.

She must have been the most determined of determined persons
She was focused on the future that lay before her then
She made the choice that she thought would bring a life
Devoid of the poverty she had grown up in
I hope she lived to see the favor that she imagined

Because the black hole she left threatens daily to pull me in

You brought me here but you don't want me
You made me but you won't care enough to stay
You should have given me a chance to be
You could have shown me how to love

Got No Dog

Got no dog no pickup truck no cowboy hat nor boots
Went to school got a Master's wrote books of poems
But my kids say I'm a hillbilly anyway so here we go

My great great grandpas were farmers and brothers
You can figure what that means to me
They weren't schooled in writing but they knew how to plow and plant
When the country went to war they took their only trip to beat up general
Grant
They followed Lee's army up to Virginia to fight a rich man's battles
They did all right until Grandpa Stanton got shot up in a Pennsylvania field
Where crops should have been growing on that July afternoon

I don't think Harry ever got hurt. He mighta took a walk before the fightin'
really started
We don't know for sure maybe he did some farming up there but both of
them came back
no doubt with stories to tell for the remainder
Of course their kids got married
And became my great grandparents
That turned out ok but for the occasional tic in my cheekbone

No stories succeed them but their son my grandpa Benny made a few
Like when he shot Al Culler in the face for trying to bail
Then spent five in the pen for master minding the car theft gang that Al had
snitched on
Until he took a walk like grandpa Harry right out of that prison and changed
his name to keep outside
But grandma Treva divorced him for being gone so long

11

I guess living the farm life just wasn't for him as it had been for all the generations before

He mighta liked his fedora and his three piece suit too much because he never went back to the ground

Of course everybody in the county knew where he was

But no one ever thought to tell the law

So he lived out his days selling various products

Some of which actually mighta got delivered as promised or not

With grandpa Benny gone, my daddy got a new brick laying father who didn't care much for kids

Pop said he would get a lickin' regular and found that most things were forbid

He started liking girls a lot early and I think that didn't go over well

His new daddy and grandma Treva figured he'd be going right to hell

So he left school and became a brick laying assistant to his step dad

Which just made things that much worse

Because he got strong and tan and didn't care

And spent a lot of time on his hair

And even though he wasn't part of the educational system he still found various school girls pretty much around the clock

My mom was still in high school when she found that I was on the way

Pop had only seen her a time or two because there were many others out there with which to play

So I guess he thought my coming made it time to pay his debt to his nation

She told him and he ran away and joined the Navy

And that was pretty much the end for them

How Did I Get Here?

We are a part of the world we walk in
As green as the corn stalks lining each row
We live because life springs up here
We have all we need for us to grow

My daddy and his daddy before him
Worked the farm that gives our family life
We help to grow the livestock and the crops
It is the source of our comfort and our strife

But how did I get so far from the place I know
Why would I shoot these fellas I've never seen
I was taught to be good — Whatever that can be
And not to hurt anyone — No matter what they do

Now the red clay is for someone else to tend as I march away
I've left it all and now I'm forced to roam apace
Somehow I've come to a meadow way up north someplace
It looks greenly familiar but smells like death today

The balls fly by like buzzing bees
I hear the screams when they land
Men fall just where they are
There's an empty space where they stand
I might be next to be mowed down
Not much longer above the ground
I reckon I need to get out of here now
I will no more be bound

'Cause the government came and got me
And every male who could hold a gun
And now we're lost among ten thousand boys
Who make the hard ground as their bed

The farm back home would have kept us alive
But this land will swallow us whole
Which ain't no big trick — we've got so puny
It's hard to keep my trousers up —we're marching scarecrows all

They lined us in front of strangers dressed in the blue they wear
And armed with rifles just like us
We shot them as they stood and both rows screamed with the blood lust
That rose with the taste of powder in the air

Then in the quiet after the killing we thought about what we'd done
The sounds of fury and the sour smell of bodies exploding all around
And we saw the red streams flowing both ways from the killing
As they settled in pools all along the ground

And the balls fly by like buzzing bees
I hear the screams when they land
Men fall just where they are
There's an empty space where they stand
I might be next to be mowed down
Not much longer above the ground
I reckon I need to get out of here now
I will no more be bound

Yesterday we lit up the world — it was a thing of wonder
Created our own stars and terrible rolling thunder
The morning brought a bright summer sun
But we made it cloudy by noon and for the rest of the day

I'm going home where there's daylight and life rises out of the ground
No more killing just for glory nor a rich man's gain
If the yankee rifles don't end me, then I'm walking on back home
And hope I may recover and make my life my own again

I've no dog in this fight — this Pennsylvania meadow should be planted and lush
I'm afraid we've ruined it for the future during these brilliant July days
But in the end we're running toward the shooting when we ought to be
running away

The balls fly by like buzzing bees
I hear the screams when they land
Men fall just where they are
There's an empty space where they stand
I might be next to be mowed down
Not much longer above the ground
I reckon I need to get out of here now
I will no more be bound

The Lord said we're not to murder
No killing for the sake of it
I'm dirty tired and hungry
And I feel like I'm oh so wrong
So I'm leaving with the dawning and I'm walking home
If I leave with the morning I'll get there before too long
Just got to light out real quiet and hope no one notices I'm gone.

I'm doing things I know I'm not to do
I can't be a soldier no more
The sun will be up in a minute
Then I'll look for a way to go
If the fighting comes again like yesterday
It'll be the end of more than a few

The flies bit us endless in the following quiet and kept us all from sleeping
And we considered the next day's plan to fight
As predestined as the midge's bites
In the darkness I hear the weeping
From those who will never see the light

You Wore Red Fragile Clothing

You wore red fragile clothing
You moved without stepping
Floating over a floor of seawater and pearls
Those of us privileged to observe
Could not imagine a sight
More graceful that night than you were

Your beauty it thrills me
To think that a person
The same kind that I am
Could be as special as you

Not just your body
But all that you can do
A mind so thoughtful
As quick as the light is
As deep as the night can be

Echos keep sounding
Not fading but gaining
Like the train that is coming
To run over my now
And decide what's remaining
Not sure what is happening
But I know we will be
What we should be somehow

You never stop doing
You the artist the model
Who we would all follow
If we only knew how

You the actress the mother
Devotee of Apollo
The god of music and dance,
Poems and the truth from the bow

You shape the world with your kisses
And spin it with your wishes
None of us can approach your bright star
But we are caught in your reflection
In a mirror of introspection
Which guides us to be the best that we are

Ecstacy must include loving you
I feel it coming in the distance now
And I am trying to learn just how
Heaven's not here but you are
And that will be enough for today

Echos keep sounding
Not fading but gaining
Like the train that is coming
To run over my now
And decide what's remaining
Not sure what is happening
But I know we will be
What we should be somehow

Love is God

In the beginning God is love, light, and all that is good
Nothing is beyond and God is all

Then light becomes love and good and there is no more God
Who has been subsumed by the light itself

Finally love is good and God and all there is
And the evolution of God is become complete

God is light
Light is love
Good is love
God is love
Love is God
Love is good

Southern Gothic #1

So I was visiting Pat back in Catawba County
Because I heard he wasn't doing well
He didn't feel like going out
He wouldn't even bite at my bribe of a perch plate at the fish camp
He just wouldn't get out of that La-Z-Boy
So we sat in his kitchen and listened to the ball game on WNNC
Dave was still calling the games just like he had for years

Bandys was taking on Maiden
It was the annual knock down
We hardly ever beat 'em
But that just meant we had to listen
Because this might be our year
We were hoping this would be our time to win it

And they had a commercial on the station about Burke Funeral Home
Which reminded me of Gary's monument out there
Gary was a kid we all knew who looked a lot like the TV Uncle Fester
He got teased some so a lot of times he was crying when he got off the
school bus
But he was built just like a lineman and he had a flat top just like his daddy
Who was a North Carolina highway patrolman who spent his days on the
interstate
Givin' tickets to speeding Yankees breezing through on their way to the beach
Everybody loves it at Myrtle
Just can't beat that place in the summer

So when Gary got to be a freshman he went out for football
Just like every boy who was anyone he had to prove he's not a sissy
And that August heat always beat down real hard on those first workouts
And his body just couldn't take it

Just too big and still too young to make it
So he died there in the old field house right after practice
And there was nothing any of us could do
He just collapsed like a worn out plow mule
And never said a word, the worst thing that ever happened at school

So to avoid a big ole lawsuit the school board put up a granite monument
Like a football shaped headstone with his name on it on a little rise right
outside the stadium
Where Gary had breathed his last
Because it had been a few years I just wasn't sure
If they had decided to take it down once things cooled off some
But this is what Pat told me —

The monument oh that monument well yeah they moved it
Right over to the gate going into the ball field
That they remodeled with an artificial surface
And they added seating but you got to get
Season passes anyway or else you'll be standing
In the end zone just like we always did
Yeah just like we always did

And they built a new field house and put it in the other end zone
And named it after Thomas J Foster
Because he gave them the money to build it
And so his name was up there in plastic covered lighting
Right behind the cross bar so it was in the way when they worked out

When the kickers went to practice
They would hit the letters with the football
And after awhile it read T as J F st then T F st
And then they just took the sign down

Well Tom got his money because he ran the local Ethan Allen furniture factory.
He had a big ole house out near Little Mountain
And he built a landing strip out behind it so he could fly his Cessna
That's where he and his son Lon crashed while on a landing
Something happened we just don't know what

But Tom got killed then and Lon broke his leg so bad they had to amputate it
And he didn't want to lose it because he wanted to be altogether
When Jesus comes to get him so he brought it from the hospital
And kept it in a smoker but he got behind in house payments
Because it turns out Tom had done a lot of the remodeling and bought the plane
With company money and they wanted it back which didn't leave much for Lon

So he moved to South Carolina to live with his mother
Leaving his stuff in a storage locker but the owner auctioned it off
When he stopped paying the rent and the leg was in it
So the new owner found it and decided to put it on display
So he charged three dollars just to see it in the smoker
And Lon heard this and decided he needed to get it back
So he and Caldwell the guy who bought it went on Judge Mathis
Who's on channel 4 every weekday at 5 o'clock in the afternoon
And the judge heard the both of them and gave the leg back to Lon
But said he had to pay $5,000 to Caldwell who had built a shed to store it in
So that was the end of that

But yeah the monument is still out by the stadium you can't miss it
Looks kind of like a football graveyard but it was the right thing to do
Yeah it was the right thing to do

And I don't remember about what happened in the football game that evening
And Pat won't know either because the cancer finally killed him like it will
us all someday
We'll all be standing there together in the end zone again soon enough

When You're My Age

When you're my age I hope you have someone
To talk to you and laugh with you
At the world that spins on without a word
And thinks it does not need you

VOLUME TWO

From The Palm Tree

From the palm tree
The harvest moon in full view
And imminently hootable
Nestled among the fronds
Hidden but alive and singing
The only song he has for us all to hear

Calling out in the darkness
While awaiting the sun's bright promise
WhooWhoo over and again
Invisible but insistent
In the dark of the night
Supplicant of morning

Daring the light to appear
So it can happen all over again

You Made Me Older

You made me older than I ought to be
I was a lot happier before meeting you
I don't see happiness in the way this thing ends
You've already killed all of my best friends

The doctor says you're still there
Though I don't feel you right now
If there were a way to get you out of here
I'd do anything — just show me how

Flowers drape the stone on the ground
Those who I love lie beneath

In the night of the dead
They come back to me
Tell me they're ok
And that I should not worry about them

I miss them every day
And my life is not the same
And it cannot be so
Ever again

If I could get my hands around your throat
The world would be a better place to be
Grabbing you is like taming a shadow
I don't expect to find a way to hold you down

But life gives as much as it ever takes
I can be the brilliant warrior or just the clown
I don't believe you will continue to matter
Though I'll be staring hard next time you come around

But I daily dread the sun going away
I sink as it does into the endless dark
And all those faces from my earlier life
Reach up to remind me again
Of previous joy and now's empty pain

Flowers on the stone on the ground
Those who I love lie beneath

In the night of the dead
They come back to me
Tell me they're ok
And that I should not worry about them

I miss them every day
And my life is not the same
And it cannot be so
Ever again

And it's because of you eater of the living
Destroyer of families and friends
You whose unblinking ceaseless grin
Bares teeth framed by dangling shreds of flesh
While gnawing through decalcified bones

You the vampire of future dreams
Sucking away the light of well being
Breathing out rancid pain and powered by the screams
Of those victims of your dumb saurian menace

amorphous and without edges
inconstant and ever moving
afflicting until surrender
with death the only treaty
Damn you
Damn us all

I don't care for you
Or what you do anymore.

Flowers on the stone on the ground
Those who I love lie beneath

In the night of the dead
They come back to me
Tell me they're ok
And that I should not worry about them

I miss them every day
And my life is not the same
And it cannot be so
Ever again

I Flew To Paris

I flew to Paris in October because the rates went down then.
Like the pod people at the movies, they all looked like they ought to
But when they opened their mouths — Sacre bleu!

Actually I landed in Brussels and took the train to the Gard du Nord
Stopped in the tourist center, there found a room
And walked to it without ever touching the ground

All on my college French with a Carolina twang
It was a comic rendition of Adam making hims way through the Garden
Way beyond the normal — just the way life should be

Then I floated throughout the city in a consubstantial dream
And spent a part of each day but Tuesday in the house of the inspired
Once a palace, since an added pyramid, those weeks a temple of all that is
beautiful

There was an ethereal stone goddess just out of touch
A famed smirking lady distant and exclusive
A winged and wonderful angel the epitome of power

Among all the ethereal drops from that which hovers above us all
Reposed in grace and grandeur for the common folk to view
It was a world away from the world that I ever knew

Ain't No Grass

Ain't no grass or flowers in the ground
Just concrete and asphalt from here to there
Walls and locked gates have me bound
All that moves free in this place is the cycled air

Hard time it seems is the only time
And only is the way we have to live
Until the final whistle then does blow
It's not a place of joy or humor
Harsh laughter follows those who can't stand the pain

I'm doin' time in this hostile place
Sentenced to a life
Stuck behind these block walls
Where people come and go
And lifers all we breathe alone

Many are gone now that were here before
Some I knew and stood near through the day
Others I crossed the open yard to ignore
Seems like the good ones always go away

The sun hovers above unreachable and without
Don't do me no good to watch it cross the sky
I'm stuck down here doin my own time
Ain't no weak ones no old ones here
They can't make it cause self is all we've got

I'm doin' time in this hostile place
Sentenced to a life
Stuck behind these block walls
Where people come and go
And lifers all we breathe alone

We're all bound and hopeless
Though we don't see the walls
Until we bang our heads against them
Soon what's real begins to encroach upon the dream
And we find there is nothing for us at all
But the bonds that shape our own inability

I'm doin' time In this hostile place
Sentenced to a life
Stuck behind these block walls
Where people come and go
And lifers all we breathe alone
Until the final whistle then does blow

What Was I Thinking?

What was I thinking?
She said she loved me
She gave me all she had
I took what I wanted
Then I thought I drove away

Her hair a lovely veil to hide her eyes behind
Her skin as tightly wrapped as sculpted marble
She seemed to dance with every motion
She made both our longing and our devotion

Because somehow we drove out of there together
Just the two of us
Left the party behind with the others still there
Just the two of us
Now we face the highway and the storm clouds
Just the two of us
No one else can come along here
Turns out it's not me but just we two

All was square and bright
As I felt my life pulsing into hers
I thought God looking down on me
And saying It is Good.
What it was felt ever so right
She brought me into the pure blue light

I couldn't watch her eyes and the road the same
We tired quick of the highway droning
But together we seemed to be flying
She was the inspiration of so many moments
Her eyes took up so much of my time

Somehow I thought I was at the wheel
Whenever she would kiss me
We would go faster
When she'd tell me of her love
We would just go faster
She knelt and put her head in my lap
And we went ever faster

I still thought I was driving when
She said she loved me
And we went faster
She moved into my house
And we went faster
She had babies
And we went faster

Life became a blur crouched beside the roadway
As we sped by cocooned within my car
Turned out she was driving all along
And the brakes went untouched for all our time together

What was I thinking?
She said she loved me
She gave me all she had
I took what I wanted
Then I thought I drove away

Now I want no women in my life
I've enough of puzzles and errata
I know I am not perfect
I don't need to be reminded every day

I was at the wheel, right?
Whenever she would kiss me
We'd go faster
When she'd tell me of her love
We would just go faster

She knelt and put her head in my lap
And we went faster
She said she loved me
And we went faster
She moved into my house
And we went faster

What was I thinking?
She said she loved me
She gave me all she had
I took what I wanted
Then I meant to drive away

Growing Up

Growing up in Catawba took me a direction that a city boy might never go
I didn't get a lot of attention 'cause I learned quick what they wanted me to know
Like when the sun came up it was time to be the one who made his way
Lots of work to do that had to be done before the end of every day

If it wasn't the Sabbath morning and time to go to Sunday School
Then I grabbed clothes for the field and with my brother became another tool
Ready to face the world's challenges replete with storms and rain
Just add a coat to stop the cold and let whatever seeps through remain

I was not born a rambler
I know life's a bully with unflagging threats
Too many ways to lose not enough to win on any given night
He's standing in the middle of my path with his arms folded tight

I got jeans and t-shirts
Enough for a week
White socks to last 'till I die
Stylish I'm not but I know who I am
And I wasn't built to wear a stinkin' tie

I know you talk to her
And that's ok
I don't often get to your town
If you see her out and about
Tell her for me I'm still above the ground

All those that came before me lived and died where they were born
Caring for the place and the people they would someday live to mourn
But I couldn't finally do the same and was the first one to move away
I lit out for who knows where looking only for warm and sunny days

It was my family's sesquicentennial and I celebrated it by running west
I didn't know where I was going but I knew I could go a long way before I'd
need to rest
I didn't have a map or a guide I made the highway to be my host
And I didn't stop or think again until the road ran out at the other coast

But I was not born a rambler
I found life a bully with unflagging threats
Too many ways to lose not enough to win on any given night
He's standing in the middle of my path with his arms folded tight

And I got jeans and t-shirts
Enough for a week
White socks to last 'til I die
Stylish I'm not but I know who I am
And I was not built to wear a tie

I know you talk to her
And that's ok
I don't often get to town
If you see her out and about
Tell her for me I'm still above the ground

So here I stand far from the place I was expected to be
I just couldn't give my life for the common cause that was expected of me
Sorry that I left you there alone and wondering what to do
I made the choice I made for myself and the same is open to her and to you

But I was not born a rambler
I found life a bully with unflagging threats
Too many ways to lose not enough to win on any given night
He's standing in the middle of my path with his arms folded tight

And I got jeans and t-shirts
Enough for a week
White socks to last 'til I die
Stylish I'm not but I know who I am
And I was not built to wear a tie

I know you talk to her
And that's ok
I don't often get to town
If you see her out and about
Tell her for me I'm still above the ground

I Remember

I remember lips and chin
Hung below the tip of that straight salient line that split your face
Where now after the horizontal endless plague
Only fabric remains draped and shuddered by regular breaths
Above a delicate throat
That turns those beautiful eyes on me
In a steady arc like the rising of the moon

Perhaps a day may yet begin
Where we might share each other's warmth within the same space
As we both were mysteriously supremely made
To wrap our own selves around each other until our deaths
And drape each other as a coat
Within which to live and become what we are to be
Not poison but proffered life emerging from love's cocoon

Fact and Truth

Fact and truth should not be confused as the same
One is a photo while the other is Monet
Anyone may walk by a still deep pond floated with lilies
But they will not see the truth that is just submerged
As it winks slyly at the passing form

You showed me the difference in those years gone by
Together we spoke of that untouchable force
Knowing we could never hold it as useful and supreme
But it would not matter as such is not of this life
To discover it in the unconscious moment is to be fulfilled

You can close your eyes now
You've done enough to get us both through
I'll be ok now for whatever time is left
Thanks for always being there
You've been the best part of my days and of my nights

Facts and truths lie still along the path
Like ripened fruit fallen from their source
The one crushed by the drop and sticky from its wound
The other haloed by innate beauty
Designed to last outside of this our time

I would gather the one to use for a day's repast
And admire the other for its inherent strength
The one was never meant to last
Like the bodies we dwell awhile in
Like that which goes on once the season is done

You can close your eyes now
You've done enough to get me through
I'll be ok now for whatever time is left
Thanks for always being there
You've been the best part of my days and of my nights

To know that you were and will be again
To help another lost one learn to be
When time once more begins
Makes it all sensible yet still mysterious
As is the form and color of all that is
And is yet to be again

You can close your eyes now
You've done enough to get me through
I'll be ok now for whatever time is left
Thanks for always being there
You've been the best part of my days and of my nights

I Was Never Here

I was never here
You just thought you heard my voice
An echo from across a distant hill
Since then I have blown away
Dry ashes in the wind

I wanted to be
But I could not make the choice
A wish which was unfulfilled
I was not meant to have a day
Dusk has come to make the end

Yet I have a destiny
Though the tale is never mine to devise
So it always ends just as it will
I can but follow the crooked path that goes its way
And take the rising turns with which I must contend

I Ain't Afraid

I ain't afraid of dying
I say
They say I got claustrophobic because I am
I ain't I say
Fear of the box is down at the bottom
Beneath all I know
But it ain't I say
It just ain't that way

I am
I can go all day
Never looking back or ahead
Just focused on the moment
No reason to think about being dead
I say I ain't
Time ain't my concern
I'm just doin what I do

They don't know
I see what's in here
Though I don't dwell on it
Where the sun is
Don't matter none
Til it's too dark
To see to do
Then will be time enough to lay down

I Need You

I need you
That's all the message said
Not specific as to how or why
Just the subject verb object
As simple as it gets
As primal and necessary as love is
Nothing else required

I need you
I don't remember writing it
Not the inadequacy nor the action
Yet there it is
Fear in the moment of realization
A three syllable request
When life has become too much

I need you

Did You Feel?

Did you feel what happened just then
When our eyes met?
The moment paused
Looked around and asked what was that
Nothing will ever be the same again
Now we are

VOLUME THREE

My Dad Had Apple Trees

My dad had apple trees that he loved more than he did some of us
They were icy gray and dead to the touch in winter
The cold air froze them in place stagnant and quiet
But they were secretly alive and though they seemed barren and lost in February
Spring brought pink blossoms that were born from each colorless frame
An umbrella of soft pink skin from which juicy red fruit sprung by July
They just needed the time

My dad was a Minister of The Gospel
He believed in life everlasting and that God is Love
We ate his apples and marveled that he could manage such a process
With his head so far into the sky dreaming of a place that none of us could see
While the leaves turned glossy green and shielded us beneath each canopy
And the heart-shaped fruit grew and hung as heavy as the now pliant limbs
Could hold bent just above the warm dark turf

We never saw the connection between the eternal and the cyclical
That which is ever changing always evolving into the thing it already has been
Eternal is forever but is never the same from moment to moment
Except that it is exactly the way it was last year of the same season
It is the rolling wheel turning toward its own horizon growing until the end
Which is yet the beginning of what is to be as it was and will be again
This is the way of love and it lasts eternal but it is only the same for a moment

As are we — never ending ever changing forever and ever
Amen

Ecce Homo

Ecce homo he announced as I neared the door
I could hear the droning of the conversations in the next room
The prattle of after dinner plans and tomorrow's tasks to come
Then I entered and a few of the heads turned quick toward me
Then back like disrupted chickens in mid peck
Back to their world of talk and their tripartite meal

I took my distance and walked with it to a corner
There I could sit quiet without requiring any notice
There I commune with my thoughts which go no further than my fingers.
To be in a room nearly frantic with the echoes of silverware scratching china
Where I might reach out and touch with my words another human life
But I am not included because like all the other times I do not know how to be

Maybe we were always communal in our feedings in our comings and our goings
Did we always know lonely or was it a learned consideration
There's a game here with rules above the other animals and me
One must know when to make a move or retreat to lower or to raise a glass
I was never any good at it not at this or any other of our games
My ex told me I was socially retarded before she left with her friends for the
evening buffet

The World Is Always

The world is always on the verge
Of blowing up
Of flooding its valleys and plains
All the way up to its mountain tops
Of burning down to its rocky core
Ending us all as well as our children and theirs

I just don't want to hear it anymore
I could listen all day to the words of experts and their warnings
And during commercials I'd realize I couldn't do a thing to stop the fail
I can only watch as it burns brighter and beyond any hope to prevail

Darling How Long

Darling how long is he gone for now
Are you alone in that house washing your hair
Wasting your night away
You know I'm not sure what you're waiting for
I'm here ready to spend time with you
Wanting to make everything all right
What do you say

Your eyes make me forget what I was doing
All I want is to be with you tonight
Let's spend it together playing
And with nothing between us feel what it is to be right

I don't mean to cause you trouble
But he's not here to hold you close and I am
We'll make memories for always
I can put loving warmth where there's now empty fright
Alone's a cold and scary place to be
In the dark who knows where the cries come from
Please don't send me without and away

Your eyes make me forget what I was doing
All I want is to be with you tonight
Let's spend it together playing
And with nothing between us feel what it is to be right

You know I can distract you from the world
Make you breathe heavy and forget the pain
You thought that love was there

I don't make such promises — no battle flags unfurled
Just kiss me now and I will lay you down
And we'll forget the world going round and round.
Together we may start a whole new day

You are sweeter than the first light of dawn
And softer than the dusk that blankets us as one
Which is what we are meant to be for awhile
Life is here to be taken and used
No time to waste on impossible dreams
Like the essence of the rose with the moment infused
All that could be is just what it seems
Make the choice and do as you may

Your eyes make me forget what I was doing
All I want is to be with you tonight
Let's spend it together playing
And with nothing between us feel what it is to be right

This Is Your Wedding Day

This is your wedding day
When you no longer feel alone
But half of a whole for the rest of your life

He goes up the yellow ladder you follow along
He falls into the dark abyss and you are the pledged jumping betrothed
Remember your vows are a rite of restriction
Promises that chain you to the marriage post

You've gone from stumbling to dancing but you'll be back here again
You escaped gloriously being with me
Flung off my presence, ran lightly to him
But all I ever asked was that you hold me and kiss me
Now you've a contract to fulfill rules and a promise sure to grow grim

What's he got that I don't
Among those questions that won't go away
What didn't I do that left you with wanting

I did for you and asked from you only just a kiss and a hug
What should I have done to avoid this breach that brings me sad and sadder
Nothing left to hold to or dream of now you've gone to stay
Life's uncertain and I can't understand it

You've committed your life to someone who assured you the same
Life does not allow for such consistency
If you live long then you'll regret these words
There's more to a moment's commitment than changing your name
Nothing you can do that a change in future sunlight won't make you betray

Would I Let My Hair Grow

Would I let my hair grow long and wear dark glasses
Should I cut those people out of my life
Maybe add The Black Fireball From Hell
Who smirks her ironic course through the day

That could be too dramatic a change
Given that old people don't recognize sarcasm so well
I'm too old to sleep too young to die just yet
Still given to dreams to direct me along the way

If I could do it all over again within this constant spell
Falling again Rising again Falling and Rising again
What will it be like when I do it all over again
When once more I lose the world imposed shackles and do as I may

Somehow we begin with freedom's unending chances
And lose such vision with each succeeding choice
Every day wants its confining decisions to tell
And we grow smaller with each word we are made to say

I'm Old and I'm Tired

I'm old and I'm tired and I need to sit down
But for M
The ducks will have to wait for their feeding at the pond
Nothing awaits my attention now that matters to me
Except for M

The sun may wander as it pleases
The leaves may ripple and dance upon the oaks
I'm no more interested in the breezes
Than the daily actions that fade away like winter smoke

M, you bring the life that I need to live now
More than anything I've ever had before
I'll give you all I have left to give now
And all that you are I promise to adore

I Don't Mind

I don't mind living alone
To come and go as I please
Do what I want and like most that I do
No day is more special than the rest
None is complicated by the wishes of you

Such freedom is costless and airy
Requirements are minimized
To that which is necessary
And that is each act in the moment I decide

Occasionally there is an uproar of holiday
Or a special event that interrupts the quiet
We are expected to arrive in pairs or more and play
Those are the intrusive forces that ripple my smooth flow

A life is what happens during those days as they are numbered
When I review my years I want to see actions that I chose to take
Not the left right left right of the slave or the encumbered
But dance steps grown from the soil beneath my feet

You would have me commit to another's wanting whenever
Spend my precious hours strapped down by a lonely unattended
With shared moonlight and crowded endeavors
To trade my successes to warm against a separate soul

That is not the life for me
I have given my self and been handed back dry ashes
Where a red and passionate heart used to be
I'll just stay where I am with what I have left for those days I've yet to see

The Fig Tree

The fig tree shelters the sidewalk that runs beside it
Its fragrance spreads into the street beyond its thick green self
With downed fruit lying beneath spewing red innards in heaps
The guts raw and sticky awaiting the gardener's own efforts
To bring order to its fallen state

The fog smears the city lights with its slippery self
As a dim light peaks over the cradling gray hills
Delaying the dawn and hastening the sunset
Surrounding all beneath its protective limiting shadow

Here I sit in quiet dread of the abbreviated day spread out before me
I sense the sudden movement that pushes on and as the prey's last moment
zags aside
Determined by the unseen faces that somehow control it all
Like the mysterious little sprinting men I see stumbling at every corner

I await my turn without a sense of why or where I should be going
Then I move forward within the established rules that I imagine are agreed
Never sure of my acceptance or the requisite for such a thing
I notice all that surrounds me without knowing why they are

I've heard that everything fits together like the parts of a blood red fruit
The skin, the pulp, the seeds all make a whole that feeds the hungry
An adjective that became a noun when the need overwhelmed us all
Maybe this is the end of order and the prideful response to daily life

If all is connected, then why do I walk unnoticed and alone
Where are you to draw me in and above the detached sticky heap
How can I find you to make me one who lives within the constant dream
If you can save me from this devolution then show me the way to be

What Am I To Do

Shot number one
You jumped into his bed — one bare foot visible sprouting from a heap of
tangled sheets
You tell me you don't love him like it really matters with you lying above him
as if you both are one

And another shot of
You upon his lap with a smile of adoration that makes my eyes burn in the
moment of realization
You look at him as if you're offering to be his next meal and I can't imagine
that you even remember my name

What am I to do — you said you would wait for me until I could return for you
You're out there for the whole world to see your beauty released and free
I am supposed to love you so I do but I cannot — I just can't — I can't go
on like this — I can't

Yours are the eyes I float into sleep thinking of
Yours the arms I dream of falling into every day
I don't have another reason to keep going on now
I'm left to find my self a new purpose in my own way

You Do What You Need To Do

My mother existed by giving of herself
Taking on every task for everyone
She would trade her moments for another's smile
She was everybody's mom

She filled her life with Christ
Praying and giving love to all
Feeding those who crossed her path
Doing at least one good thing a day

Standing by the big black bottomless hole
That is my companion for all my life
I write the words that keep me sane

You do what you need to do
To keep you upright and through another day

And To You

And to you my second best bed
May you sleep with fevered dreams upon it
So to learn the lessons of the only
And try to forget what never happened in life
When life was possibilities yet to be

VOLUME FOUR

Suddenly The Door Slammed To

Suddenly the door slammed to
And I was outside all alone
No one came to my rescue
I was left out there to make it on my own

She and I had been together
Planning out the rest of our lives
We had dreamed of eternal sunny weather
But then she'd started sharpening her knives

No I've learned that thinking ain't like living
You've got to get your heart into it too
One plus one is only another one forgiving
But I heard each can pull the other through

We were ok until the kids started to come
Then decisions that required choices had to be made
And always changing schedules had me on the run
And the warm light of a quiet moment had to momentarily fade

Can there be joy in such sudden changes of direction that affect the two
Is it possible to forget the now certain uncertainty of what is yet to come
Does the disappointment of the now's requirement destroy any anticipated
comfort
When everything seems paralyzed beneath the pressure of time's hard thumb

Where the air smells like a 64 Biscayne and food tastes like a rendering plant
There's no inspiration left to be used for love's long term success
The good that awaits those who stay and win back some vaguely outlined joy
Abandons those who cannot do but succumb to the day's unwashed stress

To survive, in the end you must kill your world in an act of thoughtless violence unrehearsed
Because the world around teems with life that seeks itself to be
Each will take yours if able always willing so you must strike first
It seems bloody and awful and without exception and it seems to be only to me

And then you go again alone and find yet another to help cover over the current scar
Announcing why don't you come over here and dance with me in unseen grooves
We've got enough in common two arms two legs held together by who we are
I'd love to know you better so take my hand and show me how your body moves

You say you need something you can believe in
Someone to walk through the day with a body to hold in the night
You want to be loved to be shared with to listen and to talk to
Rather than to be alone to plan to be as your own thoughts take solitary flight

You want to have a hand to reach out to and those eyes to look into
To love and laugh with forever as if real is love
Look around— growl — it all most certainly passes
My only answer is to select that which I know of

Because you feel like you're needy and ignored doesn't make you the central ingredient in this pot
Chicken beaks and feet circulate within while an occasional quill floats to the top

Growing Up In Carolina

The Cherokee chief was blue-eyed and pale beneath a many-feathered crown
He was selling tomahawks made with smooth river rocks painted and heavy
Each lashed to a stick while a tiny white label read Made in Japan

Mom and dad knew my brother and I would smash 'em up quick
Hopefully before a concussion happened or a prized knickknack cracked
It was much later that I read about the Trail of Tears
That decimated those who were made here to live and love this land

I remember delivering furniture in Maiden formed from the local trees
On the day when the creek that ran under the highway and into the woods
Was as green as the remaining oak leaves that shaded its path

It was greener than the grassy yards lining the road
Greener than it ought to be just down stream from the hosiery plant
Where an industrial dye began its quietly anomalous journey to the sea

I'd never seen anything like it in nature's fine reality
A Christmas ribbon winding itself away and beyond
Coloring its native crawfish and salamanders like wriggling pickles
Wrecking the life of our waterway and warping what I expected to see

When Roy and I had it out in the smoking room at Bandys High I beat him
until he could no longer stand
Then we went to the Boy's bathroom and cleaned off as much blood as we
could from each face
My left eye was swollen about shut while his nose was headed a different way
than it had been when we began
But we were both ok for Civics class where I just hoped Ms McKenna wouldn't
look too close
She didn't notice a thing out of place

Mad Dog 20

At a hayride out on a dark dirt road near the church where we'd always gone
Mine was a clown's mouth red and wide and my heart was beating like it
never will again

Mad Dog 20 in a cup of ice and your eyes teasing me for more
I learned to kiss that night as part of a ritual of love
A knowledge that had dwelt upon the sea floor among
The simple and juicy life of faceless beings submerged until now

Yours the lips that woke my dreaming self that showed me your mystic hidden
value
You were warmly quiescent while nudging me through the night — your
strength was in your giving
Making the body I had used to run and jump over hurdles into a tool for
pleasure beyond my imagining

The last time I saw you while crossing a road on foot
You looked down at me as if I needed badly to be crushed
It seems that the end of love is distraction
Disregard begins with prolonged familiarity

On Beer

It's part of my diet of champions like eating a bowl of Wheaties
A couple beers keeps me smiling through the day and the night
And allows me to go on past the grim and prim weary souls without

Beer withstands gravity as the free flowing thing that will
You can float above the world's misery and enjoy the rushing thrill

Same as a girl might who can make you lose track of whatever else there is
Because nothing else can matter regardless of the direction of your analysis.

Inebriation without cessation might be a little bit much
But getting there nightly while hanging on tightly is how I manage my touch

You Are A Bright Star

You are a bright star in the dark and lonely sky
A light to guide my lost soul wandering beneath
Toward the final goal while I still breathe
To maybe know at last the reasons why

I've seen your sorted colors blaze above my head
I know you are here for me to learn what is yet to do
A meeting still to clear the way so I can live in the beauty that is you
A constant love to push beyond all the fear and the thundering dread

You are the slender sunflower leaning toward the light
Drawn to the good that will show me the perfect way
To surely pledge my life to draw the magic from each awaiting day
While focused with you upon the good that is here and all through the night

What more sign do I need that everything is as it should be
What else could I know that would support my unsteady eye

She Walks In Beauty Still

She walks in beauty still beyond my understanding
Like a sound so fine that my dull ears cannot receive it
Like the bright bands of light that soar beyond my blurred eyes
A thing so delicate I cannot believe it though I sense that it is true

She is the one who I know exists to give me some sane purpose
Though hidden as she is by graceless city lights that displace the stars
By the roaring freeways whose traffic red and white splits the land
Now the population grows to hide what's special within its squirming mass

Yet I dream of her in the darkness left upon the waning of my day
Forgetting all else that stands frantically determined to stop my way
In the quiet I focus upon her ascendance from the rest that is indifferently
indifferent
As I watch her approach, I can only imagine that to her I am foolishly ignorant
To think that her compassion, her enduring love, could be spent upon me
Who is no more special than the diurnal circle that continues dumbly
repetitious to be

I Don't Understand

I don't understand why I can't see it
It should be as clear as the sun the moon and the rest
I'm sitting among the ashes that were my life
Make your bright beauty to shine down upon the gray that surrounds me
Stirring my direction with the impulse to rise

I've spun around and around in a tiny arc
The rock in the sling whirling in an ever speeding circle
Let me loose — allow me to fly into the sky
As far as you can toss me — having wound up for all these years

But for now I sit in the dark dreaming of you
It has been so long since the sun shone radiance down to me
My body your body our body — you are the promised one
Come to me now at the last— I am ready
Show me what you would have me do

Up In New York

Up in New York City and other parts near to there
They got lots of Yankees who'll tell you how much smarter they are
Than anyone you'll ever know where you live
It's been that way for lifetimes now since we lost that xenophobic shootout
That some dumbass back home did not think through at all

They came to get my great great granddaddies, brothers who had been
Working hard on the farm where they and the rest of my family had been
born for over a hundred years
Where they'd done the best they could raising or hunting down what they
would eat
Then the government man had them make their mark to go up with the
General to shoot the Yankee boys who had not yet done a thing to either of
them and to continue the horror of the black folk that belonged to the rich
men who neither fought nor shared in any of these trials at all

So after being raised carrying a load on my back because of the continuing
curse, I moved out to California where they had nothing to do with any of
that mess
Instead they had been busy taking land from the indigenous folk, and so
their livelihoods, now pointing out to me about the "cotton curtain" which is
innately evil they say — and stupid — which I can't argue — though I have
read all ten of the Bard's History Plays and learned that we are not the only
ones who let testosterone get in the way of probity
But these westerners were never part of it at all — in fact they were nothing,
no part of the killing or the racist chants
So now they need to fill themselves with righteousness knowing only that
what happened happened somewhere else or no place and did not involve
them at all

In the great battle that rages upon this desert place and all
While the reigning pietists struggle mightily to destroy the evil that exists in all
The demons seem winning daily even as perfection stains the eye blue sky
And eventually those who were never anything must yet be deprived of the sun and all

Sometimes

Sometimes
The current of reality
Pulls my sense of place and self up by the roots
And for a lost moment I am free

Granddaddy Ben

Granddaddy Ben stole cars in a gang of his own making
And shot ole Al Culler when he threatened to turn them in
Fast and mean, taking an eye and a big chunk down to his jaw
But not his mouth so when he could he still sang like an angry canary

So granddaddy went back to the pen where he'd gone once before
And then was alone at night in the quiet and working on county roads all
day long
Grumma filed the divorce papers soon after he was locked up again
That's how she made it clear she might want help with the kids but not
from him

When Grandaddy got out he never went back nor called
He drank AA bourbon and danced down at the auto repair shop on Saturday
nights
That's when the just scrubbed concrete floor was covered with women and men
Who had nothing more to do and nothing worth giving to give

He thought anything would have been better than going back to that farm
The place where the family had been chained to the dirt as far back as he knew
Where going was hard and little mouths were always hanging open with need
And as much as you got was never enough and the pickings were always real
thin

So he worked at various jobs to feed himself and never stayed any place long
And didn't look back but made himself complete within knowing he'd no
doubt soon be gone
Having abandoned the place and his family which he knew was his
unforgivable crime
Saying "There are a lot of broken hearts in here ... even four or five years is
a long long time."

I Didn't Want To Fall

I didn't want to fall this far
I always thought the end would come
Long before my self was worn
To the thoughtless clicking of chicken feet

The clerk at the chain store gave me a senior discount the other day
I didn't ask for it but when I saw it pop up I didn't know what to say
Of course I'd like to spend less but how did she decide that I'm an old man
I guess when you're twenty, anyone over thirty must look older'n sand
Right? I said, "Right?!"

But I love the dream that follows me still each night into untethered release
Rent and credit card debts are forgotten with all wrongs blocked by peace
Replaced by cool evening breezes and beauty beyond this place
While a new found love purely refined allows an unflinching embrace

Here beauty raises her perfect head awhile and offers startling eyes and smiles
Without doubt or fear dissolving all weariness and ending the endless trials
Yes, I want only to be with you as should everyone who slips through the
open door
You are a shining facet that has not been seen here among our kind before

But upon rising I feel the wind has changed now blowing at my face
My aching body slowed by gravity's pull and all the years invested in this space
A storm now looms upon the near horizon and the dark rushes on fast
As I cough and stumble my way through the day imagining each to be my last

My life requires a considerable rearranging to find a reason beyond the release of each night

I need the promised purpose to keep me going through the never warming light

Please to make this happen for me to give to you before I am finally and completely gone

To pass these selfish intensities that I cannot keep myself forever to be running on

I Feel Temporary

I feel temporary
As if the elevator door is about to open
And my world will become an expected
But previously unseen room

VOLUME FIVE

Now It's There

Now it's there. Now it's not
Time's grind (not endless but unstopping) made it disappear
Now it's here. Then it's gone.

The backyard bird of paradise is ablaze
Its flames reach the sky
Abandoning its own quietly green body

Leaving below the why torched by the summer sun
You're the only person here that I want to talk to
Pourquoi pourquoi pourquoi

There'll be a half dozen or so will show
If it don't rain much
Bring a cover to hide yourself from the gray mist

There are green sparks in the bright beam surrounded by the darkness
Flashing for a moment then not
Not then then done

The leaves are gone from the vineyards
The plants are gnarled and spent
No more wine no more glory

Now it's there. Now it's not.
Pourquoi pourquoi pourquoi

The hidden creatures spill out once the lava cools
Digging through the crust to face the green framed sky
Fucking and gobbling up all others close enough to touch

Just let go don't overthink it
Not much chance of that
The end is near

A solstice is the conclusion of each process and the beginning of the next
It brings lightning to ignite the seeds to growth
Thunder to loosen the walls of obstruction

Now it's there. Now it's not.
Pourquoi pourquoi pourquoi

This Old House

This old house has plumbing that whispers in the dark
Nightly it can only moan and complain
What had been in the light is now veiled and not to be displayed again
It dares me to listen and howls sometimes
A low rising discursive rush of sadness
Trapped within its old iron cell

A moonless night of distress echos through the rooms
Incomprehensible while I sense the loneliness would seep itself out
The misery felt through the sounds of sudden trembling
Amid pipes vibrating as it rumbles approaching louder
Menacing within but trapped now forever

When the sirens cease a moment
And the music stops to catch electric breath
It demands to be considered
What led this haunting spirit to this place
And why does it cry in the night

To ignore it is to give up on understanding what lies there
As it describes its ancient woe to one with boundaries less visible
Who listens closely interpreting the context
But avoids the latest plea for help — such is beyond me
To release this watery spirit from its tightly sealed submerging tomb

You Took My Home

You took my home and all my things
But you could not make me bow

You put my family
My reason to be
On a bus pointed I hope
Far far from here

Now is the time to focus on evil
To learn to kill
To take a life
All the lives that rise against me.

I turned my cheek already
There's nothing left to give
Until the war is over
No one left can live

Just Keep Running

It's been a long time coming
Whatever may be the climax of this strife
Surprises keep on piling up
But I've kept moving all my life
Always I'm becoming
Ever working toward the ending of this life

I don't know where I'm going
Don't know why or when or how
Going as fast as I can knowing
Nothing's ever coming —
It's always and only just as it is right now

Just keep running
She told me ever
As time will never stop
No end is yet within my sight
Just keep on running
And try to outrun the everlasting night

Just keep running
Don't stop or you'll be left right there
Just keep running
Not a moment — not any moments — left to spare

Dad's gone
Mom's gone
Brother's gone
They're all gone now
The last day is coming
I can hear the whisper as the final morning moans

So I may as well just stop running
Time to do the right
Stop this frantic running
Turn around and draw the light
Just stop running
Stop and hope to put it all to right

Mistakes there are — always something wrong
So stop the running
Take time to mend the errors of a life
Stop now this running
I'll not outrun the everlasting night

It's been a long time coming
Whatever may be the climax of this strife
Surprises keep on piling up
But I've kept moving all my life
Always I'm becoming
Ever working toward the ending of this life

I don't know where I'm going
Don't know why or when or how
Going as fast as I can knowing
Nothing's ever coming —
It's always and only just as it is right now

Molly's Backbone

Molly's Backbone starts as a quick exit off of the paved road out of Terrell
She's as twisted and crooked as a tangle of black snakes in a 50-gallon barrel
She's the dirt road that leads her lovers out of this world and into a never
ending dream
Imagined more than made, like she was created to run through not around
the standing pines
Zigging and zagging she throws up a sandy cloud like a storm over the distant
Sahara
Layering the shadowy trees and hanging sandy tarps over the kudzu vines

Once a deadly Ford 390 4-barrel attacks with spinning tires and frantic
fishtails
Blowing blue smoke mixed with red dust in the swirling explosion caused by
the metallic whale
And roaring like disruptive thunder with the maxed out accelerator screaming
Then it vibrates the earth with consequential violence
Scattering anything on legs into the dark of the surrounding woods
Lost and gone and forever leaving behind any sense of sanity or silence

Just keep it between the ditches they cry
Spinning every direction of the circular dial
Creating hysterics among the watchers as the loosened gravel flies
Within the scene of movement so maniacal

Sometimes they have to pull one back onto the chest heaving road
Whatever they need is done for and by themselves according to the lost lovers code
The cops and workmen don't go near to the dusty swinging stream
Because there is no reward only a risk of eternal loss of good
And not worth the chance of never coming back to pavement
Here where the sudden and unexplainable roar echoes throughout the dark wood

Ain't no tar back here just an endless layer of dust
Waiting to be stirred, a latent cloud before it rises like a final shout
To blind the sight of all that are
And block the exit of anyone intentionally wandered off and suddenly wanting out

The back way home is a highway graded and tarred for travel
But Molly's Backbone is for when you're lost and have no thought of ever going back
For a challenge offered freely that can only be lost
And those who have entered in will never know or consider even the cost

Then hidden by the haze and after the racing, the Ford is parked between the pines just off the shoulder
All that will remain by sunrise are the scattered tissues and used condoms sticky with the night
Sheet metal gone and dusty boots no longer
Still the air remains fuzzy in the morning light

It might have rained up in the town
But it is never muddy back in there
They all choose not to see the where
Because the seeing can only drag the lot screaming lost in the dust filled air

A road should go a place but Molly don't
You can get onto her but there's no egress
You think you'll figure it out but you won't
Like a wrong turn in the darkness, there's no way out of this

It's never quiet for long
The silence when it happens is foreboding of what's to come every day
There is no leisure
Only the anticipation of the danger on its way

She Is Tall and Circular

She is tall and circular
And she spins as does the earth
I can only follow in her constant wake
And never assign her worth

When she looks in my direction
I am frozen in the moment
When she speaks within my hearing
I can only dwell upon her comment

Learning about love with her
Has given me a chance to be
Everything is become now new
She's opened me up to see

M is all my reason
Why I am and where I'm going
Not for just this season
But as long as life is flowing

Rebel Yells

Both of my great great Grandpas fought against the invaders
Those who would take their peace and their lives away
There was no place to run from the bands of raiders
They could only crouch and hope to live through the day

They were farmers both who lived upon the land
Eating what they raised or shot for food
Sharing with their neighbors, lending a hand
Or asking in turn for help to feed the family brood

But when the local government men came to take them
There was no place to hide — none to run to
My grandpas had to foresake their own during the coming mayhem
From the plow to the rifle they went — nothing else would do

I was sleeping upstairs and missed it
I was asleep and I missed everything
Now the critics all mistake them
So easy to damn the dead
What need is there to shame them
They sleep now — their tears have already been shed

They never owned a man nor wanted to abandon their kin
But a rifle was not new work to their hands
At fifty yards both could light a match stick or wipe off a horse fly's grin
So too they would put an end to the charging men's plans

They were bound by their oaths and rode with the Northern Virginians
Fought their way from their farm north through many thickets and oak
Marched through the blue coats and killed so many with nary a complaint
nor opinion
And slept beneath stars obscured by the rising of the battlefield smoke

I was sleeping upstairs and missed it
I was asleep and I missed everything
Now the critics all mistake them
So easy to damn the dead
What need is there to shame them
They sleep now — their tears have already been shed

They fired musket balls big enough to take out yankee limbs
Until the powder and the balls ran short and out
Then they tossed hard dirt clods and sang loud their hymns
Hoping to ensure the charging yanks some doubt

Finally before the end they were down to their rebel yell
Which would curl the standing hair on most men
Sounding as if it rose its way straight from hell
Much cold work for awhile at least as the enemy closed in

YeeHaw!

I was sleeping upstairs and missed it
I was asleep and I missed everything
Now the critics all mistake them
So easy to damn the dead
What need is there to shame them
They sleep now — their tears have already been shed

In the end they walked their ways home from Pennsylvania
Bloodied and with only thoughts of home which had never left them
No more need to bow to the grandiose pursuits of others' egomania
They found again their farm and never again let another's dreams possess
them

I Was A Young Man

I was a young man sure of both his feet
Who could do and be as much as he ever liked
But nothing arrived without an effort
Always requiring a breath-speeding fight
But it's all headed off now as easy as can be

I've been going uphill all my life
Now I've reached the top of life's transcendental arc
And it's all downhill from here as I'm headed on and out.
To find that after all this I may not even have left a mark
All that remains is to count out the sum of what may be left behind

What I've been given is leaving me every day
The wrinkles are leaving my brain emerging onto my face
I just can't get used to this intolerable rodent race
No I never got comfortable in this unexplainable inexplicable maniacal place

My mother prayed for my soul and thought me a slacker
Because she had more rules than I could ever follow
I just turned away and moved on, having thanked her
While she got so palsied by the stress she couldn't swallow
And I found a world outside that ignored her nos and came along with me

Love stands here guiding my way on through to the finish
Her hand in mine I do not fear the remaining path ahead
She has always been here and never lets my hopes diminsh
I know the pain that comes along is meant to counter joy with dread
Like left to right and up to down as we spin on out of here

What I've been given is leaving me every day
The wrinkles are leaving my brain emerging onto my face
I just can't get used to this intolerable rodent race
No I never got comfortable in this unexplainable inexplicable maniacal place

All the old folks are gone now and I'm the one that's left behind
The rules have been learned and forgotten along the way
And I'm here waiting with the sense that the stars are now finally aligned
Now to end all my efforts my dreams and questions as I start to fade away

What I've been given is leaving me every day
The wrinkles are moving from my brain emerging onto my face
I just can't get used to this intolerable rodent race
No I never got comfortable in this unexplainable inexplicable maniacal place

The Secret

I know something you don't — I know how I will die
The monumental secret voiced — in a sterile room
Soon a day is coming — without me here to see
A chiseled stone tells strangers — when I used to be

Do I reveal the secret — do I pray for peace to come
My thoughts are swirling round me — again
No answers can I leave you — 'cause days don't bring the why
My minutes were never right — To move, breakup, or die

I was hard and fast before — the kids began to be
Which left me soft and smiling — loving them's easy
They're what I'll miss the most now — losing's hard for me
So I must phrase my last words — to leave a memory

Do I reveal the secret — do I pray for peace to come
My thoughts are swirling round me again —
No answers can I leave you — 'cause days don't bring the why
My minutes were never right — To move, breakup, or die

And just as winter smoke does — I rise and fade away
From this hurtful world and — all its short-lived pain
Only silence stays here — and nothing more from me
Gone from here as days dawn — and life spins on its way

Do I reveal the secret — do I pray for peace to come
My thoughts are swirling round me again —
No answers can I leave you — 'cause days don't bring the why
My minutes were never right — To move, breakup, or die

Upon Viewing Luhrmann's Elvis

As the slender boy rises to the light
Of his music's brilliant melodic flight
A creation fed too by the dark beat
Of a heart which twitches him head to feet
I am reminded of the thrill brought to
My life with each note of the songs he'd do

With a sneer like a smile tragically spurned
While revolving within the world's twists and turns
Through him we felt the black leather of life
The rock king himself swept up by the strife
Choosing passion over false modesty
Making decisions to spite those who bully
He stands upon the others so to see
And holds those lost who have helped him TCB

Lord, give me the sense not to pretend to be wise
But let me feel that world which will love he who tries.

The Thing I Am

As to the purpose of the obsequious bitch whose hand I took and sought to lead along the way
Who rose to overwhelm my life for thirty years, all my time, my thoughts, my self
Until the day I walked away toward that which I knew I should have been heading all along,
She never admitted nor even saw me as the thing I am.

VOLUME SIX

I'm Dropped Over The Side

I'm dropped over the side and rocked by the wake
Fumes float just above the water and burn my nose
While I shake the cold film from my eyes
The boat goes on shrinking toward the horizon as I lose interest
And begin to think of all that I have had and been

Life started with every need met with the asking
Now I bob with the tug of the earth without and alone
Supported for awhile by sea water of which I am
That will soon pull my body down
To merge with its unseeable silent deep

There was a day when I as a child of my father
Walked unencumbered over ground that seemed
To go on as far as I ever could know
Then I was alone and the pathway disappeared
And my legs sunk beneath me and I feared that I might drown

Someday it will be warm and dry— the cold still water will be gone
And life again will be as it was but I don't know when that will be again the
norm

Never Going to Mombai

I'm not going back
I've met them all and talked it through
Nothing more for me to say or do
I'll find a quiet place and try to heal
And then I don't know what
I'd like to feed the ducks from the bench
Down by the always reflecting pool

But I can only move ahead
I'm to face the world as I am
And do and think the things I can
It's not a choice for me after all
We are to move on through
Light the candles that count the years
And follow the path until we fail

Love me because I'm a good person
Love me because I am here
Love me because I am hurting
Love me and hold me dear

Destiny fate or god are here
What we're to do and where we go
Is already planned to ensue
Go on ahead and don't look back
Yours the life written to be
Yours to listen close each day
And then to find the way to act

As it is its the way to be
The end will come on anyway
Nothing to fight against or dare to say
You're not the author of your story here
Follow the plan as its given
Do the right you know to do
The distant horizon will become clear

Love me because I'm a good person
Love me because I am here
Love me because I am hurting
Love me and hold me dear

What's coming approaches anyway
Take it as it comes knowing it's for you to face
Keep on moving toward the coming of the day
And when it's done you'll have found your designated place

Love me because I'm a good person
Love me because I am here
Love me because I am hurting
Love me and hold me dear

Back When The World Was Black and White

Back when the world was black and white
When the visible like all life existed in opposition to itself
Before color began to expand our choices
Bringing the confusion of tint —
Life was much more innocent then —
The options limited so the actions easily defined
Now the secrets of simplicity are overwhelmed —
I've no idea what is the wrong and which is the right

My children have no interest in the monochrome
They see life's bright freedom as it is unquestioned
While I stand behind and wonder
What change in the lighting must confuse me next
Mine began as a world of symmetry
Balancing sides of optics — pride and shame
Life and death — everything a shade of itself
Now daylight blinds my path with its blush

Then the light upon my mom's perfect eyes
Showed through to her calculating soul
A focused beauty beyond color
A spirit untouched by threat since
Maybe you had to be there
Like a story from a land now disappeared
Where a heroine relies upon her knight to reestablish order
As the disruptive dragon's heart must be removed

Harassed by red threatened by blue
A green one and a brown one
Turning me the uninvited monster itself around and away
But I comprehend the positive and the negative
With up and down left then right and to to fro
Why does the light require such study
Why can't I see what others see —
A world of beauty and inexplicable sights

They Slid Off Your Paper Gown

They slid off your paper gown
And placed you gently upon the gurney
Your hair drifted to hide your eyes
And across you the linen rolled out and down

Then they wheeled you away
Out the door into the flowing endless hallway
Where I was not allowed to follow
To a place I feared you might stay

They cut you open juicy ripe tomato
Your skin no longer held back the flow
Of your warm and consequential life
Which spewed out like human fruit upon the table

They picked out all the rotten spots
And put you back a little less than before
Still pulsing within softly mellow
A static self with death now sewn into your thoughts

Then sent you back supine and silent
Your vision blocked by benumbed eyes
Your self forever changed by the required loss
A trade settled for some added days of quiet

We Let Our Lives Mix

We let our lives mix as converging water
Both streams flowing unimpeded through each day
From her I'd seek direction as the faithful servant
The chivalrous southern boy throwing his ego away

For many years we spent living like this
Sharing our lives as one among the many more
It was our turn to be lovely and gracious
For awhile just she and I je t'adore

But not always could I submerge myself
Not every moment be the giving half of us
And finally when the silt rose up to fill the delta
Flowing slowed to stasis and then we were surely lost

So I'm sitting up here thinking about it all now
I watch it happening again but cannot look away
In a world where the only thing that survives is love
Still go and love one another the best you can each day

In the moment just before the roller coaster ride begins
All loaded up with high expectation marked by sweaty hands
As you clutch the cold steel protective bar just think of her anyway
Hang on tight while the speed becomes as much as you can stand

With arms flailing a life worth living though strapped in
To go both high and low as faster and beyond any plan
In a world where the only thing that survives is love
Go and love one another as you may each remaining day

Every Man Imagines Loving You

I hear that you are splitting up
That he wandered again and you said enough
I don't know what place he is going to
Who could be so blind as to turn his back on you

You are so beautiful gracious with a faithful heart
Your movements your glance are those of classic art
You personify that which is beautiful and loving
Being with you would bring the worth to every day
What's he gonna do when you take his world away

You're another species above us shining from the sunny blue
I am filled with wonder as the world waits we all gaze up to you
I know how incredible how most perfect you are
With love beyond measure you are truly a star

Every man imagines loving you and most women too
Loving the chance to have your focus for just awhile
Your love your counsel your ever perfect smile
To describe you requires words that have yet to be said
You are the most beautiful creature any god ever made

I understand male urges and life's need to roam
But not to betray to lie to give away your home
Shame on such ego unchecked and unbound
So tell him such behavior makes him alone
Just wipe away your tears and then move on

You've lost love before but that doesn't ease the hurt
Every time is the first time and there exists no pain worse
Such rejection doesn't kill us no matter how much we wish it
Heartbreak only maims but then love is never quite the same when we give it

Every night I wish the salty tears that you cry
Could be me so that I might touch your perfect face
All day long I look to see if you may be near to me
If you were the world would become a perfect place

The Loving Night

We lay long breathing washed sudden ashore
As the salty foam uncovered us two
And the outside warmth returned
Sand in the bed never felt so fine
And all that was left was dreaming again
Of the place we had just already been

Your eyes all I see and leading me
To share with you all I might know
You are so lush and proudly made
Just as I knew you would be

When you asked what you might do for me now
I saw Destiny smile broad and wink
And so I said love me
You can love me
Please love is all I ask
Look at me — I'm here for you
Don't forget the things we said and did
The loving night — It could not have only been a dream

But those legs so long so straight as you move
More graceful than the moon that arcs the sky
I'll never be over you
Never forget the things you said tonight
Nor the touches that took place in between
You the author of all that is was or can be

I wonder where you are gone to
And how I got left behind
It was the night of lives in conjunction
A time that shows us how to be

When you asked what you might do for me now
I saw Destiny smile broad and wink
So I said love me
You can love me
Please love is all I ask
Look at me — I'm here for you
Don't forget the things we said and did
The loving night — It could not have been only a dream

I believe everything you do and say
It's all as right as the air that I breathe
But now you're not here
And the only thing that's changed is me
The ink upon your heel
A weakness looked through into another life
Only visible when you turned to leave
Your perfection all I knew 'til you walked away

When you asked what you might do for me now
I saw Destiny smile broad and wink
So I said love me
You can love me
Please love is all I ask
Look at me — I'm here for you
Don't forget the things we said and did
The loving night — It could not have been only a dream

It could not have been only a dream

I Know That You Can't Stay

I know that you can't stay here
Your thoughts are already down the road
Don't leave me to decay here
Not sure I want to bend beneath this load

Just tell me where you're going
And when you'll be getting there
I'll figure out how to be blowing
Ain't gonna worry about what to wear

I've never been away from here
But wherever you are is where I want to be
Being with you where you are is better than any other place
Let me know and I'll find a way
To see you there

What do you call that disease
Where you ain't ever happy where you are
What happened to end your ease please
That kicks you down the road so very far

I knew it when you kissed me
The distant lights reflected in your eyes
I only hope that you would miss me
And want me beneath the newly rolling skies

I've never been away from here
But wherever you are is where I want to be
Being with you where you are is better than any other place
Let me know and I'll find a way
To see you there

And if you decide to leave without me
I guess I'll have to start wandering around
The world ain't that big anyway
I know I'll find you when I can
Yours is the life I want to be near
Your beauty your grace and those eyes
Keep looking out the corners I'm bringing you my self as a surprise

I've never been away from here
But wherever you are is where I want to be
Being with you where you are is better than any other place
Let me know and I'll find a way
To see you there

M Today

Do you know why I'm here today
Why the years have brought me to you
How I might need to see you now
After all this time without ever knowing
Your name

It's time to replace with beauty the emptiness that chills my bones
Sing me a melody slowly building until I can hear the truth of it all
I need to know a reason to lean toward these sacred tones
You can bring it you can and together we can love to take the fall
Together

In the bright light we rise and descend humming as we do
With heaven opened circling the vision that is you
In the light of your loveliness your grace and your charm
Touching your easy body and then sliding on through
You hold me as I take you into my arms
For we

Slowly building focus as our bodies begin to flow
Slowly moving upward finding love as we learn to go
And slowly, slowly, slowly arrive at the point of ecstasy
Then quickly quickly love the feeling of being you with me
Always

In the bright light we rise and descend humming as we do
With heaven opened circling the vision that is you
In the light of your loveliness your grace and your charm
Touching your easy body and then sliding on through
You hold me as I take you into my arms
For we

Nailed to a board like a supine Christ for all
A scar like a zipper now separates me from my self
Dividing all that was from what is supposed to be
I can only watch languid as you become the savior of me
My life is liquid only — I direct it as best I may
And trust this paper thin cover which is good for yet another day

In the bright light we rise and descend humming as we do
With heaven opened circling the vision that is you
In the light of your loveliness your grace and your charm
Touching your easy body and then sliding on through
You hold me as I take you into my arms
For we

On The Floors Of St John's

On the floors of St John's
Where the sun shines calmly outside the fray
Where the surgeons decide who can be helped to stay
And the nurses hang the bags and draw out blood every day
While the patients hurt and struggle to overcome the cure
That can be harder than the illness for them to endure

Because it lies in wait for everyone
No way to stop it or avoid its deadly coil
If you can live without the part it's ruined
Then you can go on with the scars and the horror of it all

I'm stapled together like an old wornout doll
Can't yet walk on my own or even stand without a fall
I don't know when I can do anything or be who I am
Everything in me is mad at the world that did this to me
The docs would blame it on my life but I've never sought to die
As if I poisoned myself by living as we've all been taught to try

Because it lies in wait for everyone
No way to stop it or avoid its deadly coil
If you can live without the part it's ruined
Then you can go on with the scars and the horror of the hurt

I don't know if I can do this anymore
My life ain't supposed to be over with so little done
The future which had been so clear is now a roiling blur
So it looks now like I will not be the one

It lies in wait for you as well
No way to stop it or avoid its deadly spell
If you can live without the organ it has destroyed
Then you can go on with the scars and shun for now the silence of the void

With Nowhere Else To Go I Went

I loved her as a young man
She took my breath away
She asked that I be with her awhile
But I could only see the day
I grew soon distracted
And we parted for awhile
Now it's been a lifetime
And the world has lost its smile

I've got to find her again somehow
I think she'll remember me
Having her to hold at night
Will give a reason for me to be

I grew up in a one light town
I knew everyone who was there
From cousins 'round to school chums
Never a stranger anywhere
We'd trade out a girlfriend every week or so
Knowing that we could do it all again
When we got to the place one had to go
Not love not yet just a partner to hide with from the rain

One day I'd had enough of the place
So without much thought I lit out for the territory
I took my car my stuff and all that was attached to my face
Living out my own picaresque story
Heading west the road seemed long and full of promise
As I zigged and zagged without map or plan
I had no goal to be honest
Just to be somewhere I knew no other man

I stopped in Yocnapatapha's home
And walked the house of Bill my muse
He'd gone already so it was all dry as a dog's gnawed bone
But I could sense the outlines of a life made of blues
So I drove across the Memphis bridge west toward heaven
Over the river that split the place
Where the sign said No Tolerance to be given
So I turned north and hurried to make some space

I made it past St Louis' arc and kept the river to my right
Then crossed to Hannibal's muddy shoreline to see
What it might have been like to grow up in a place small like mine
Running and telling lies and always feeling free
I watched the river flowing by the muddy banks
A welcoming wet border to swim and play in
A way to escape when it was time to say goodbye and thanks
Needing only a homemade raft to float away in

Then I turned left and went across the plains states
Maybe if it's your home you want to live there
Folks look as if the land is spinning their fates
Like the hot summers and hard cold they'll need to bear
I knew that was not the place for me to be
Small towns they had and I knew not a soul
But the flat land and long horizons without a tree
Did not fit with my search for a freedom loving goal

I've got to find her again somehow
I think she'll remember me
Having her to hold at night
Will give a reason for me to be

I drove until the road ran out
And the sun set across water endless and cold
So I guessed this must be my new home
And with eleven million people it ought not grow old

I met her in a bookstore at a mall with no roof
She wore a Louise Brooks bob like a little boy
And dressed in a shifting smock that hid her truth
I couldn't tell what might be there to enjoy
She looked me up and down and noted my twang
I guess she didn't think much of people from down there
We didn't exactly hit it off with a bang
But before long we were holding hands and laid all secrets bare

I wasn't sure that she was going to go with me
But then she invited me to come on in
And with nowhere else to go I didn't think but went
Dear Lord I later prayed I am a foolish drunk
Please help me to know why I'm here after all the time I've spent
And where we're going now and will she be coming along
Is she the one I was really searching for to complete my song

And a voice said to me
She will be the morning that shines upon your hopes and dreams
She will bring focus to all the good that lives within this place
From here to the far horizon she will go beyond all the means
And hers — hers is the one with the bright and shining face

So I've found her somehow now
And we'll make memories enough for all to see
Having her to hold at night
Will give the reason I need for me to be

The Light Of The Ever Traveling Moon

When can I see you — I'm getting out real soon
We could meet over by the bus station diner
And ride together beneath the light
Of the ever traveling moon

VOLUME SEVEN

I Know You're Angry At The World Now

I know you're angry at the world right now
That you've held your temper close for long
That it's been eating at you — you're about to bust
But think a moment about what is happening
Even though you're surely the one we should trust
Do you win as your screams and harsh words rock your core
Its anger tears you down but love will make you more

Lift us all with your wisdom
Show us the ignorance of not giving up our love
You are always right here in the daylight
You know the direction we should go to rise above

Don't lose yourself in the garbage that surrounds us
Do what you know is right calmly and with care
Give us the example that speaks truth to what should be
Those of us who listen will follow as we dare
Some will remain lost and left behind to cease to grow
You can't take everyone with you
Although we'd all be better off if you could you know

Lift us all with your wisdom
Show us the ignorance of not giving up our love
You are always right here in the daylight
You know the direction we should go to rise above

You can share both anger and loving
Which do you think will make life better for all
Don't tell me you've given up caring and want the world to fall
You can kick all the asses and take all the names
But a loving reminder may work just the same
Instead make the world better than you found it
Spend each moment seeking the path to make a better way

Lift us all with your wisdom
Show us the ignorance of not giving up our love
You are always right here in the daylight
You know the direction we should go to rise above

The Darkness Of Your Smile

The darkness of your smile leaves me wondering if I should just go
Your beauty is no less than when I first felt the tugging of your eyes
But now I'm not sure enough to take my gaze away
For fear you'll be gone and there'll be nothing more to see or to say

It didn't take long for your heart to rise into my view
In the moment you arrived, I found I lived only to be with you
But time erodes what were tall mountains and indescribable love
And as the clock ticks I see that you may no longer approve

Holding hands and looking into your eyes that do not look away
Walking in step as both move the same way
Always arriving always becoming never wanting to leave
What more can life bring what better reason to breathe

Your welcoming me when I arrive as my best friend
The cuddling in the nighttime as if the darkness might never end
All the ways you gave yourself to make me feel special
Are memories now that I wish might be again

I'm sure it's because of me and all my unopened doors
Because I never deserved such love and joy
But I miss your attentions just the same
And don't expect to ever find another love like yours

Holding hands and looking into your eyes that do not look away
Walking in step as both move the same way
Always arriving always becoming never wanting to leave
What more can life bring what better reason to breathe

Close your eyes and it can all look like it did again
Let me dip into my heart and find a way to make us anew
Whatever faults I've shown let me try to explain
There's no life no reason no way to be without you

Holding hands and looking into your eyes that do not look away
Walking in step as both move the same way
Always arriving always becoming never wanting to leave
What more can life bring what better reason to breathe

I Saw You With Love Lighting Your Eyes

I saw you with love lighting your eyes
Your arm in his walking together within a crowd of other people
I saw you with a smile as if you'd won the grandest prize
You strolled past the others all watching you shining gleeful

It was your day even as they all are
Built to show you as the bright and glorious star you've become
Each hour finds you with another adventure
As we all stand enamored of your life to come

Don't
Just turn around and look at me
You know it's not for us
You have already gone
And left me to go alone and make somehow a new home

I had thought to be a part of your days forever
To lay together beneath the brilliant shady tree
Dropping sweet red grapes onto your lap for pleasure
Loving each lazy moment as it strolls on by us so free

Not sure what happened how the weather could turn so hard
The leaves are gone from the now sad shade tree
The grape vines bare while the summer sun still shines with no regard
And you you have moved on to another and without me

Don't
Just turn around and look at me
You know it's not for us
You have already gone
And left me to be whatever I maybe am

What does the world bring and why
How should I look at a future of without
It was always your love that I thought would save me
But now I see that I alone must make my world come to be

Don't
Just turn around and look my way
You know it's not for us
You have already gone
And left me to be what I can yet become

The Rains Came and the Winds Blew

The rains came and the winds blew
The houses shook and the lawns went unmowed
It changed everything about all that we knew
It was the day the water flowed

We saw it on the news before we learned to be afraid
They showed a map that looked like we were in its way
It was growing stronger as its path was simply laid
And we watched closer as its approach seized our day

We brought in the lawn chairs and loaded the Prius
We lit out for the freeway thinking to find a way
Toward higher ground and maybe a cousin who'd keep us
But the streets were impassable so we would have to stay

Instead we locked everything up and moved to the middle of the house
We turned on the local news channels of the portable radio
And I listened in the growing darkness to the reports with my spouse
And the wind began its roaring and the rains came on and did flow

And it sounded like the sky was truly falling
And the rain became a sideways blustering sheet of water
And the wind blew loud as if it were calling
Us wolfishly to experience its wrath and the imminent slaughter

So we huddled and prayed for delivery
As the sky went black and the house rocked and trembled
And the shingles began to release amid an onslaught like artillery
And there were no non-believers that night unless some had dissembled

Then the local freighter sounded as if it were bearing down
Of course there were no train tracks for miles away
And as the final roar swept around us calling us to drown
We felt the house give up itself and end its long years' day

As it began to tumble up and down ended and began again
We were spun against the walls in turn and lost perspective of what as we
rolled
As we banged against other objects turned loose to fly and strike us then
And all I remember is that only fear remained as we had lost all sense of
control

And the water raged and the house dissolved into the flood
We bobbed at the whims of monumental energy we had never imagined
Eventually we were down more than up and the water became warm with
blood
And what were left of us wouldn't be enough to examine

Then the storm went on spraying our DNA north across the country
And when the sun returned they sent drones to assess the damage
But the lost were reduced to numbers rather than to relate the horrors bluntly
Because it would be more than the living remainder might be able to manage

And lives must go on despite the world taking us apart in violence unbridled
And there must be a future possible regardless of our hostile earth mother
So those escapees must push on as if they are still entitled
To ignore the horrors that are thrown daily without conscious reason at
another

You're The Most Beautiful Creature

You're the most beautiful creature any god ever made
More graceful and more brilliant than any of us could be
You can't hide it or deny it because you're built to be displayed
And we stand in awe as you show us how we all should be

You make life altering decisions seeming on the fly
You're smarter so impatient and you think we're holding you down
You think you've figured it without really understanding the why
Then like us the unknowable reaches up to alter each plan you've drawn

Flying by the seat of those beautiful pants
Never sitting in them you only know how to dance
You can't slow down there's no way to go home
You just keep going like you'll never ever ever be alone

You should lean on other normals to moderate your pace
To slow your speedy ascent so the bends don't dare kick in
To keep you from breaking harsh barriers with that perfect face
And to clean up the mess that you're just about to slip in

I know there's good looking rich guys ready to pounce
Who will promise you the moon and all of the stars
I'm not as smart as you but I'll love you with every ounce
And there'll never come a time you need to hunt me out in bars.

Flying by the seat of those beautiful pants
Never sitting in them you only know how to dance
You can't slow down there's no way to go home
You just keep going like you'll never ever ever be alone

129

Just think about me a minute will ya
You know you're always on my mind
I can't stop it as your being subsumes my every day
And all of my nights and all of my time
If you want me close then all you need do is to say
In this world every moment is likely yours anyway

Flying by the seat of those beautiful pants
Never sitting in them you know only how to dance
You can't slow down there's no way to go home
You just keep going like you'll never ever ever ever ever ever ever ever ever
be alone

I'm Trapped Here In The Wilderness

I'm trapped here in the wilderness
While the world spins on its way
She's not going to make it and neither am I
Life will not last us — we must surely die

It's not tragedy — it's process
And this life is likely to be born again
And once more disbursed but individual
Advanced by facing the future inexplicable

Everything that's born must end
While the purpose is to go down swinging
With someone new dedicated to love along the way
Shouting a last goodbye to end the final day

We've marched not in sync like a military review
But side by side with hands held loosely
And smiles for the future while pushing aside the murky past
We watch each other's eyes and pray that they might last

I can only be the one you know me as — ready and aware
We are of a single heartbeat and never should turn away
I look over my shoulder and no one is back there
'Cause the rest have dissolved in distance as do the days into the air

Just me and you to do it for as long as we will be
We know that time is coming to take away our lives
But now is long enough and someone watches to see
That the progress of our actions is worthy to survive

So no more looking back and no more dreaming away
Now is the time for action to do what we've to add
And build upon the foundation that waits for us today
A lifetime spent in being lifts a world beyond all we've had

The Rites Of The Walking Are Many

The rites of the walking are many and vast
We assert our power beyond those who are without
Ours are the prayers to be answered
Ours the consciously conscious demands to be met

Anyone else should be prepared to bow
As our requirements are pushed to center
To support our own needs and desires
We intend to take all that we can get

If you are not one of us the peripatetic mass
If you have not risen to be as we are
Then you will take what you are given yet

Learn to accept what we deign to offer
And know that your life is unnecessary
And you unwalking extras will be easy to forget

All Right Then Young Man

Come over here and tell me your story
What dreams have you decided to follow today
What is it that will lead you to your glory
How can I help you to clear the roadblocks away

Because that's why I'm here now and always have been
Alive to be for you as you hit the unscalable walls in your days
To show you the path that you have yet to see before you throw in
The means to climb as always while your life builds to full blaze

You'll do what you're supposed to
Nothing else will matter in your life
Coaching will help focus to bring you
Through days filled with unexpected strife

You'll be what you were built to be
The results will be there for you to see

Tonight Is Coming

Tonight is coming
Can't wait 'til it gets here

Tonight will be the night
Tonight tonight I'll be with you

Limping sun drop yourself on down
Can't start 'til you're gone away

We need colored lights surrounded
By the shadow of it all

It's already determined
Our life our needs our day
No reason to worry
Just go and get her
We don't write the story
We live it each in our way

Yes You Can Stay

Yes you can stay
Let's get rid of all the others
I'll send them on their way

Come here to me and I'll hold you
And you imagine such a life as mine
Just remember to do what I tell you to

Ain't no love involved here
No connection that outlasts the rest
Just keep looking at me while I let you be near

Sure you're number one and will be all night long
And in the morning you'll just need to be gone

Get on and leave me alone
Don't expect me to love you
To give you the time of the day
You're not the one I'm gonna hold to
When the dark fades away you can just go

I saw you among the others and thought you might do for awhile
You're shiny and clean and young
Hang on if you can to that expectant smile
Who knows maybe this night will someday be sung about

To Reach Another Day

The lone sun crawls across the sky
To find a place before the dark
Not to lie in open spaces
Where menacing eyes can make their mark
Since the light giver does hide during nighttime
My hopes may not find the way
But I still feel the need to reach another day

I have been here so long so many
Always the center holding tight
The one you could always rely on
To make sure everything would be all right
Never losing what might matter
Always going straight to show the way
In order for us all to reach another day

The ones I've lifted have soared on now
Flying above and out of my life
I search for a reason to keep on going
To stand while the lost are still so rife
Unlike the one I've been holding to
I'm no longer steady on my way
So it's getting harder for me to reach another day

The world keeps circling on while I slowly
Cease to move the pieces on the board
I remember you standing beside me
Si tu pouvais lire dans mon coeur,
Without you I await the fanged and hungry
Who no doubt will send me on my way
Making it unlikely I will reach another day

Since the light giver does hide during nighttime
My hopes may not find the way
But I still feel the need to reach another day
I've always felt the need
I can't get past the need to reach another day

Age Has Turned My Hard Lines

Age has turned my hard lines to butter
Like the mountains melt into the sea

I can no longer do the things I once did
I am not the person I used to be

But I am something else now
A hollow shell that bows with the wind

Who rests daily for the final journey
So to be ready to meet the end

VOLUME EIGHT

He Always Walked With
His Head Out In Front

He always walked with his head out in front
Like he was late and needed to hurry back
He was always looking straight before
Often missing the life going on daily to the sides

I supposed something had happened in his youth
That had stung him mean and to the bone
Which had startled him to resolve not to be hurt again
So now he moved too fast for anyone to harm

He was my dad and he loved hard
I cared for him as much as a son can do
He was the strongest man I ever knew
And his final words to those who could hear him were
You oughtn't to treat a fellow so

He ran his own business and never stopped to rest
He was always planning while on the move
He only made eye contact to see if you were listening
While you were still absorbing he was off to another place

I never knew what made him so intense
Mom wouldn't say why he could no longer sit and think
She hid whatever disappointment had taken away his joy
And would speak only of a world of light and love — so mom

He was my dad and he loved hard
I cared for him as much as a son can do
He was the strongest man I ever knew
And his final words to us were
You oughtn't to treat a fellow so

Once I caught him looking toward the river
As if remembering something from a long time ago
He was fingering a hat that he was not holding
Poised as if to leap away from me and this place

But then his eyes came to focus on me and the building
He owned and built himself over the years
He turned and the day took him again
I never found out what past event he'd just relived

He was my dad and he loved hard
I cared for him as much as a son can do
He was the strongest man I ever knew
And his final words to us were
You oughtn't to treat a fellow so

He took the close held memory with him
Buried it in the same stainless box
Now they lie together in the dark and secret
And I wonder if he ever saw me at all

He was my dad and he loved hard
I cared for him as much as a son can do
He was the strongest man I ever knew
And his final words to us were
You oughtn't to treat a fellow so

It Is A Disease

It is a disease that has infected our world
Crossing oceans mountains and rivers wide
It robs us of breath and balance
Suppressing ability stealing direction

It burns through conscience and values
Turns the focus inward rejecting love and compassion
Sets the eyes ablaze and triggers the finger
Dooms the weak the small the unguarded

It personifies the saurian menace set to kill
The horrible threat I had only imagined in the dark
Gobbled up by the ever hungry never agreeable fever
Suffocated and dissolved within a heartless soulless beast

Now the thoughtless menace rises to strike us
Staring silent while we look away unconcerned
But then darkness is all and the light can never return
And the gaze remains unblinking from the center of the righteous path

Such a deplorable ending comes with no warning or threat
It just rises where naive persons forget that evil can grin
And speak of saving the needy while swallowing them whole
Who takes all we are and all we know back with him underground to digest

Throwing up a few bones maybe sinew beneath the blindness
With nothing ever more to show of love or any kindness

I Tried So Hard To Be The One

I tried so hard to be the one everybody thought I should be
But it never worked for long because I could not go those ways
I have a life like all of us but it's made to fit just me
And I must live it with the guidance of only my destiny

I've found the path sounded out by the whisper of my maker
I've learned to listen with my heart to tell the turns I'm to be taking
I'm east to west as predetermined fate directs my every way
And before each darkness I hope to end rightly every day

Listen close to hear the knowledge to be found
Find the answer carried quiet by the breeze
See the day turn toward you and nod the way
Sense the instructions written in the stars to keep you off your knees

So I left the ones I started with and went upon my lonely quest
And found a different world that met me as it would
And I have lived each moment as it came to me
While I walked the new laid path step by step between the rest

It's a scary task to trust the universe to provide each need
But those come along to help create what I may be
And arrive then one by one to make the places right for me
To do the things I am made to do and to become finally freed

Listen close to hear the knowledge to be found
Find the answer carried quiet by the breeze
See the day turn toward you and nod the way
Sense the instructions written in the stars to keep you off your knees

I've watched my friends ignore the way that leads to their own peace
Thinking they can make a life that rises without a focus of their own
Only to lose their path in the maze of choices that blocks their way
And their frustration goes ahead leaving only loss and a wasted day

Listen close to hear the knowledge to be found
Find the answer carried quiet by the breeze
See the day turn toward you and nod the way
Sense the instructions written in the stars to keep you off your knees

I Am So Sorry For You

When I was little the fields and the woods went on forever
I could walk and run for as far as there could be
And never find a wall designed for stopping me
I was not fenced in nor were there other bodies in my way

I could ride my bike on the road at the driveway
And not be blown into a ditch by a frantic herd of cars
I wandered the world without fear of others
And every day invited me out to explore

I am so sorry for you — you won't get to see the things I saw
You won't feel what I have felt — you'll have your own world
But it won't be like mine — it's not the one I came to love
Your world will be forever alien to me

And the sun and the moon they did not hurry across the sky
Their movements were slow and steady and time always waited for me
And I never got tired of moving always going and coming
And the world gave up its secrets as I came to see them shine

But you are fenced into a crowded pen like cattle at the end
No room for elbows not enough air for breathing and water has a price
Your world is limited by all the others who are milling about
And you are just another in the throng trying to make it through the day

I am so sorry for you — you won't get to see the things I saw
You won't feel what I have felt — you'll have your own world
But it won't be like mine — it's not the one I came to love
Your world will be forever alien to me

But then maybe the world has not changed
My focus may now be only the issues of the day
I am no longer little and new — my eyes do not light up at the sunrise
A thunderstorm with all its power is just an inconvenience
And people around me are no longer a mystery — I seldom consider them at all

I am so sorry for what I have become — I no longer see the things I saw
I don't feel what I once felt — I have lost my own world
It won't ever be mine again— it's no longer the one I came to love
This world has become alien to me

Welcome

Welcome welcome — glad you got here
Find a spot and hang on out
But watch to see what's happening next
You're gonna have to keep it up
And no one's waiting for you to come

Hey
I'm glad you're down to see us
Everything's just for you
Turn yourself loose now
Find someone to hold onto

Come here to get away
To take just what you need
It's gonna be a brand new day
We're here to take the lead

Welcome welcome — glad you got here
Find a spot and hang on out
But watch to see what's happening next
You're gonna have to keep it up
No one's waiting for you to come

Hey
Tell me what you want now
Show me how you go
There's no holding back now
Can't keep going slow

Lay it down take it up
Make it to the top
Only going up now
Ain't no time to stop

Ain't no aint no aint no
Ain't never gonna be another time to stop
Take it up lay it down
Make it to the top
Only going up now
Ain't no ain't no ain't no
Ain't never gonna be another time to stop
Ain't no time to stop
Ain't no time to stop
Ain't no time to stop A'int no time to stop
Ain't no aint no aint no
Ain't never gonna be another time to stop

I'm Glad I Exist For This Moment

I'm glad I exist for this moment
For the time I may spend with you
There's no other reason for me to be here
I can't wait for another day with you

Will you give up eternity for me
Will the few days remaining be enough
Let me be your sunshine
The love that gets you through the rough

Give me the chance to prove my worth
Let's make the dream become reality
I'll hold your hand to make the day
To display the life that you deserve to see

We must answer the call we are given
To create a life that makes our paths to cross
How we can be that which we were made to be
To make memories to be remembered and never lost

You were born for this — we were all born for this
Follow the direction you're given
Ignore the other ways — take the pain as well as the solace
To be found in going the way that you are driven

We will remember all that was
Before the end comes to us again
Not the end of all that is
But our end of this chapter of the song

You may fulfill your duty now
As the battle of days is renewed
Follow the opportunities as they are laid out
Become what you were created to be anew

I can bring you into the light
We will walk together shined upon by it all
And you will rise so brightly as the world
Follows to touch your brilliant self

My lady the girl of my dream
Hold my eyes awhile in your gaze
I cannot move without your approval
I cannot kiss you unless you wink me into your days

Your beauty and the grace that goes with it
Combine to make of you the perfect person to be
You can make your self the idol of the living
The dream of all those who soon will be

Some things are certain and others will be as they should
Nothing is ever wasted — we are to be as life guides us
Listen to the faint insistent voice — it's the way to find your destiny
And you will find a way through the ever tightening truss

Too Old

They tell me
You can't do that
You're too old
You'll break your neck
They'll shoot you like a horse on his back
And that'll be the end of that

They keep saying
Don't run that race
Your day has come and gone
You'll lose anyway
Dropping out along the way
Will just make you sad

They tell me every day I'm too old
So you know what I do
I do it anyway
Just the way I wanted
Without being wise or safe
You don't have to like it
Just don't stand in my way

Because it'll break my heart if I don't

They ask
Why would you want to go to the dance club
When no one your age will be
They'll just look at you and laugh
As you fall behind their newly practiced moves

You can't keep up with that stuff
It ain't the way it was
And even if it were you're not
You need to stick with your own kind
Maybe sit around the edge

They tell me every day
I'm too old
So you know what I do
I do it anyway
Just the way I wanted
Without being wise or safe
You don't have to like it
Just don't stand in my way

Because it'll break my heart if I don't

Stay away from her
That girl is fast and fun
You can't do that
You got too many years behind you now
She'll outlast you and leave you in her dust

I ain't gonna stop
Not until my breathing does
You don't have to like it
Just don't stand in my way

They tell me every day
I'm too old
So you know what I do
I do it anyway

Just my way

Well I'm still breathing so I can't stop the beat
I'm going on now staying on my feet
I do it anyway
Just the way I wanted
Without being wise or safe
You don't have to like it
Just don't stand in my way

Because it'll break my heart if I don't

I Was Raised In The Chivalric Way

A girl light and fragile walks uncertain
Through a door framed by jagged knives
A slender girl looking for a break in her life
Finding a small bed inside a blue room
After a sudden shift in the conversation
She's swallowed headfirst by a grinning crocodile
Who gave her money to cool him for awhile

I was raised in the chivralric way
Saying yes ma'am and opening doors
Wishing y'all have a good day
Taking my shoes off to care for her floors

Standing for ladies because
Asking for her side of things
Taking her word for what's wrong
Ready when needed with my roadhouse swings

Sexual power is a blinding white light
In the moment of an unveiled male threat
But looking for control in sex is pyrrhic
Which only lasts until the climacteric
After the orgasm it's already gone
And then the true strength emerges
The hormone's pull dissolves as it purges
Between consent and abuse the lines are blurred
As Y pushes the beast beyond "no" which is the final word

I never knew such behavior
I got daughters now and think it's a sin
If you're a Harvey you need to back away
'Cause you're gonna hurt some
Won't be worth the momentary tingle in your skin
Did you come for me
Yes ma'am I am

———————————————————————————

Then I heard of Me Too
I found other kinds of men in our lives
Ones that are bullies and creeps when alone
With unguarded girls even other guys' wives

Ain't no excuse for behaving so
Can't blame hormones or a need to be
Now victims tell of forced kisses
And I have to shake off the dark that's on me

———————————————————————————

The swaying bridge of desire won't carry duty
Don't be thick — Who said you could touch such beauty
It's not her fault when the Y consumes all that you are
Where flattery is the shallows and won't take you very far
Only subjects can love and care for one another
While objects are left being only the other
Your spear becomes a pruning hook as the war for dominance is over

———————————————————————————

I never knew such behavior
I got daughters now and think it's a sin
If you're a Harvey you need to back away
Cause you're gonna hurt some
Won't be worth the momentary tingle in your skin
Did you come for me
Yes ma'am I am

Flailing don't help — when a calm answer can make it right
Instead stepping through the minefield of street cred carries its fright
Such cruelty don't mean a thing because no one has control
Life brings the chances — use them as solace for your soul
Because that's all you get and all that will keep you from a final fall
Or you'll go to a place where only boys will be
Your touching there will be passed around for free
Your spear is now a pruning hook as the war for dominance is over

----

Never talking back
That's where momma began
Giving help to the needy
That's what it means to be a man
You don't abuse any lady
Young or old rich or not
Don't touch her unless you mean it
You're making a commitment of all you got

I never knew such behavior
I got daughters now and think it's a sin
If you're a Harvey you need to back away
Cause you're gonna hurt some
Won't be worth the momentary tingle in your skin
Life was sure a lot more fun before you creeps
Did you come for me
Yes ma'am I am

I see misogynistic feminists lining up to set empowerment's tone
Feminism of all isms is the one that should mean we needn't be alone
Your spear is now a pruning hook as the war for dominance is over

I Was Raised In The Chivalric Way

— Lyrics

Key — A BPM — 105

I was raised in the chivralric way
Saying yes ma'am and opening doors
Wishing y'all have a good day
Taking my shoes off to care for her floors

Standing for ladies because
Asking for her side of things
Taking her word for what's wrong
Ready when needed with my roadhouse swings

I never knew such behavior
Got daughters of my own
If you're a Harvey you better fall in
It won't be worth the tingle on your skin

Then I heard of Me Too
Talk of men without lives
Feeling real big when they touch
Hurting girls alone even other guys' wives

There's no excuse for such harm
To blame her for what she may wear
Holding her down with a snear
And I have to shake off your doubt that I care

I never knew such behavior
I got daughters of my own
If you're a Harvey you better fall in
It won't be worth the tingle on your skin

Grinning crocodiles won't get too far
Who said that you could touch her
Careful or you'll be penned up with boys
Where you could become her

I never knew such behavior
I got daughters of my own
If you're a Harvey you better fall in
It won't be worth the tingle on your skin

Don't abuse any lady
Young and poor or not
Don't touch her unless she says so
She'll let you know if she cares 'bout what you got

I Sure Do Love You

I sure do love you but I don't know who you are
Your lips salty and full of the sea
The curve of your back rolls as a calm ocean wave
The depth of your moans echoing through the room
Your kisses a warm deep bed from which I want never to emerge.
You take my breath my will my love my want

What's left of me well ain't much
You're the girl of my fantasies but I don't know who you are
I see only you but you have not yet found me
My reality is become blurry as you fade into the silence
Looks like you're dancing and purring so I must be dreaming of you again
Where you are is become a mystery to me

And I want you and I need you
But I don't know how to please you
Not like any other man to do the things he can
I can't cry 'cause that's not a thing a man can do
Now you're bound to say goodbye but I've got to find you first

The darkness was brought me by a butcher who took my life and left me
walking around
I don't know how to say this can't find a way to please you
I've wanted to all my time here but I'm not here anymore
Goodbye to hopes and wishes — I hope he doesn't live to do this to another man

I live in an iron trap of limitations pumping the air in and out of me
In exchange for breath I am stuck within this armor
I cannot reach out or hold you ever close to me
I only see your back as you walk away into a world no longer mine to see

And Now

And now I am alone with dread
I think I'll stop looking back to see
And focus on the straight ahead
Where life is full of joy yet to be

Age ain't no great thing
It doesn't take you to the top
It's a necessary evil to bring
Each day's learnings piled high nonstop

And by the end the memories are lined up
In a narrow and consecutive tunnel of events
Which for those days left can be matched up
With the familiarity that life tends to present

And when you look back far to the expansive past
Where time falls away and remembrance is a meadow
Where the first and the last are there among the rest
You'll find me rolling around in them between the hedge rows

What Do You See

What do you see in that guy?
I know he's tall but what's the point?
A giraffe's long too for reaching leaves up high
Though people generally eat while bending at the joint

I can't see another thing to recommend him
Maybe he's funny in a sad way but I'm not laughing
He's got nothing going so why befriend him
And no good reason too for photographing

Here I stand another one of the silent herd
Your eyes focused beyond my ordinary face
I've tried but cannot reach you with my words
As here I stand among those chewing constant in this place

While your beauty shines like the bright beacon on the hill
And I'm as blind as ever wondering about you still

It's Too Late

It's too late now to say I'm sorry
It's too late now to make amends
My nights are no longer very starry
Each day reliant upon "depends"

VOLUME NINE

What A Life

He met her in the valley held her hand and fell in love
They discovered brilliant places that became theirs to make life of

Soon they were one mind and body always together always there
And neither ever wanted for the other would forever care

What a life it is
What a wonderful wonderful life it is

Holding close in the evenings with their own heat shared in place
Hand in hand through the daylight nothing more beautiful than the other's
face

Days became months and those turned into years
Their dreams were born and grew and were constantly up and down the stairs

What a life it is
What a wonderful wonderful life it is

He watched them become persons of whom he was unquestionably proud
While every day of all those years was uncontrollably loud

The sun rose ever faster and their lives began to fall away
Their walks together were shorter and the wind blew on colder than they
could take

What a life it is
What a wonderful wonderful life it is

Then the night came and it was time to sleep so all the dreams did fade away
And each went on where we will all go on to live another day

What a life it is
What a wonderful wonderful life it is

Please Don't

Please don't let me fall in love — I just can't
Please don't make me love you — I don't want that
It's too late for me to love you
I don't know how to make you mine
I don't even want to know you
I've gone way too far past that line

Once I could have done so
I could have loved you beyond all things
Once I would have shown you
What makes the world's great moments sing
But we're not going back there
Those days are dead and they are gone

Please don't think I need you — I really don't
Please don't believe that love works — it really won't
It's too late for me to love you
I've been through this all before
I don't know how to prove to you
Time takes away what you once adored

Once I could have done so
I could have loved you beyond all things
Once I would have shown you
What makes the world's great moments sing
But we're not going back there
Those days are dead and they are gone

I've lived through love and hung on tight
I've felt the joy of love's bright passing light
But nothing stays in this unsteady place
Too hard to run together in this unending race

Once I could have done so
I could have loved you beyond all things
Once I would have shown you
What makes the world's great moments sing
But we're not going back there
Those days are dead and they are gone

I've Never Been The First

I've never been the first or the last
I'm the guy who came in the midst
And steadied your life with mine

I unwrap our days one by one
Hoping for designed surprises
To make it all worthy to last

And you here with cares unexpressed
With love leading through the midst
Life with you is the promised land

If you decide you don't like to share mine
Don't worry much because life will change
Without notice or request but with cause

It's destiny not disease at last
No cheeks will turn in the midst
Facing toward the progress of mine

Hand In Hand

Hand in hand through the bright lit day
Side by side down the sandy shore
Eye to eye as we pass this way
I could never ask for anything more

I wake up with your arms around me
Don't want to move beyond your reach
Yours is the unmatched beauty that I see
Such grace and artistry you always teach

It was always M
It always was
The dream of a dream
A life beyond a life
We have the direction
We know what to do to be

And your love sustains my life
Yours is the purpose I'm here to find
Melting into you removes all strife
From you exudes a glorious state of mind

Kiss me whenever— hold me as tight as you please
Don't leave me without you never ever
I know life holds no guarantees
But we should be loving and living forever

It was always M
It always was
The dream of a dream
A life beyond a life
We have the direction
We know what to do to be

When we meet she will kiss me up against the wall
I'll feel it like I never felt before
Like I knew nothing it will be a whole new day
I know we'll meet — we have to meet — someday

It was always M
It always was
The dream of a dream
A life beyond a life
We have the direction
Now I just need to meet her to be

The Pilgrims Hunched and Ragged

The pilgrims hunched and ragged move forward at their own paces
Some quickly as if late to a predetermined place and time
Feet certain and rhythmic
Others maunder unsure if they are really going or why

Their little lives are surrounded by threatening sleep
And interlarded with dreams unrelated to their journeys
Being unsure which obstacle to challenge or avoid
They cannot know which direction is the right one after all

My confusion once fogged every movement
Like walking into the tule all hope with dangers concealed
But now internal sussurations blow clear my pathway
And prompt me forward to feel the promised warmth of tomorrow.

Nobody's Listening

Nobody's listening and they never do
I might as well be a corpse dangling helplessly
And silent in the front closet

I spout tales told with hotly flowing lava words
Channeled downward through the coruscated ridges of dead rocks
Past withered tree framed memories desiccated by inattention

I hear myriad voices limning daily routine forgotten or replaced
I bear uhs and contradictions within the moment's spaces
And decide to turn askance to deflect the wounding interruptions

I've been ignored stepped on rendered invisible and discouraged
No one sees hears or cares about the existence of what I know
And rootless I cannot be

Doctor Told Me

The doctor told me you know you may soon be done
Boy you need to go out and have yourself some memorable fun
Because time is finally running out

If you stand still it will leave you without anything or anyone
And you'll be stuck standing quietly and coldly where you are alone
Without the days to do the things you should

But you keep showing up and leaving me again
Your life so dramatically inclined
I can only stand here and feel me falling more behind

I'd be a lot closer to the goal of this tragically comic journey
If you were here and holding on hand by hand with me
I'm here as always wondering what now to do

I know it's not easy taking and giving all that lovers are to be
Working toward a consequential ending that only I seem to see
But it's what I'm asking and all I need from you

But you keep showing up and leaving me again
Your life is so dramatically inclined
I can only stand here and feel me falling more behind

Maybe you could try once more
Know that I promise to be for you
That we can live love's next and final encore
Kissing one another each and every day through

But you keep showing up and leaving me again
Your life is so dramatically inclined
I can only stand here and feel me falling more behind

I Have A Song For You

I have a song for you
I made it up alongside the road
Not sure what I'm supposed to do
But I have a song for you

I heard you say goodbye again
And left me laying there alone
Don't know where I'm going now
But I have a song for you

I hope you find what you want
And that your life goes as you plan
I cannot give certainty or smiles
But I have a song for you

It all meant something before
I could find comfort in your eyes
I don't think about that anymore
But I have a song for you

The days now are much longer
No conclusions ever are
Nothing matters anyway
But I have a song for you

I wonder if you ever miss us
How close we held ourselves at night
Do you ever think of what could be
Now I have a song for you

Something special was tomorrow
It hovered above with promises to bring
I always thought we'd make it through
Now all I have is a song for you

The Bumps Along The Way

I don't love you
I don't care at all what you do
Go wherever you want to
Take what you like and fly away

No I don't love you
You never meant much to me
I know I told you I did
But it was a lie given easily

There's no aching to loss
Just a steady thump in my chest
Might be the beat of my heart
Or it could be the bumps along the way

I don't feel any pain
Your leaving is not raw agony
That changes words into knives
I'm not hurt — I don't want to die

After you are gone
There may be moments of darkness
But the things we did won't haunt
Being alone forever that's what I want

There's no aching to loss
Just a steady thump in my chest
Might be the beat of my heart
Or it could be the bumps along the way

The trouble with alone
That's not what's wrong with me
I'm as happy as I've ever been
There's no scorching pain within

Once I thought life was designed just for us
Our fates were tied to love and success
Now just I stand upon a bridge high above it all
And long to plunge into the cold dark water below

There's no aching to loss
Just a steady thump in my chest
Might be the beat of my heart
Or it could be the bumps along the way

Maybe a Cartoon Anvil Fell

Maybe a cartoon anvil fell on her head
Not sure why else she's staring at me now
Sure if she sees me surrounded by stars
Then that could be an interesting show
Maybe the flying sparks could light me up
Like a saint in a diorama
I the reliquary of the martyr
With jeans and Chuck's and scraggly as I am

Maybe she sees something I can't
A personal being beyond the obvious slob
Perhaps a depth hidden within that only a keen eye can detect
I only hope that's it since my shallows tend to stretch out
Into the dark
Or maybe she isn't looking at me at all
Perhaps she's been blinded by life's hard and constant fall.

It's New Years Again

It's New Years again gray and cold
Don't want to go out into such gloom
An environment pushing me to old
Limiting my day to a lit warm room

Is this a portent of what's yet to come
Will the approaching hours turn me inside
Do I think back to where I came from
Will I slink into a welcoming corner and hide

I've so much left I want to do
I should be focused now on finding you
I need to wander whatever world remains
To push fate's process until it complains

I guess facing toward the hostile moment is for me to do
Springing myself forward to gain a final acceptance from you

I Seek Angels

I seek angels every day
When I find them I look the other way
I don't need them with me just yet
But I know I will
And I want to know they're there
For when my time arcs to sunset

Printed in the United States
by Baker & Taylor Publisher Services